THE FUTURE OF THE WEST

THE FUTURE
OF THE WEST

BY

J. G. DE BEUS

Harper & Brothers Publishers

New York

WGE

CONTENTS

v

Contents

THE FUTURE OF THE WEST

The contents of this book represent exclusively the private views of the author; no official or Government opinion is involved.

Is Western Civilization
Coming to an End?

A̲s̲ ̲o̲u̲r̲ civilization grows older, its scars deeper, and the horizons of history wider, there has arisen an increasing desire
to assess the place of this civilization in history, in order, if possible, to draw certain conclusions with regard to its future. Yet
this interest remained little more than an academic pastime for
philosophers and historians until a few decades ago. We took it
for granted that our civilization would continue to dominate the
world, that it would grow bigger and better all the time, that it
would continue to bring about increasing prosperity and ever
higher development of the human mind.

Today we find one third of the earth's population imbued with
an ideology directly opposed to that of Western civilization; in the
rest of the world its value is being challenged from within and
without, its very survival doubted. It is no longer a question of
amused speculation what our world will look like two hundred
or three hundred years from now, but one of grim reality as to
how it will look to our children, perhaps even to ourselves, a few
decades from now. H. G. Wells painted a gloomy picture of
Everytown reduced to rubble in the Western world by 1960;
George Orwell evoked the obsession of a rigidly totalitarian society in 1984; and the Western citizen who has the courage to

look somewhat further than his garden fence notes with horror that strong forces are at work to make these predictions come true.

Thus what had before been an object of academic speculation has turned into a matter of life and death; the question which had been perceived by the eye of genius before World War I, but which then seemed of mere theoretic interest, has assumed a character of ugly urgency: is Western civilization coming to an end?

Do we enjoy the bitter privilege of being chosen by fate to witness the crumbling of this majestic structure of Western civilization, as we have witnessed that of Coventry cathedral? Will the throbbing activity of crowded New York be replaced by the desolation of a depopulated city of half-empty apartment buildings and streets with weeds knee-high? Will the towering skyscrapers of Detroit and Chicago be reduced to a shambles like the hearts of Warsaw, Berlin, Rotterdam and London? Shall we see Paris invaded and ransacked by barbarian hordes as Rome was once by the Vandals? Will our children be able to live in a world in which life will still be worth living, or will they become human robots directed by a distant dictator through the tentacles of an omnipotent and omnipresent state machine?

In short: can our civilization by pulling itself together rise to greater heights yet, or is it doomed to a rapidly approaching death?

These are vital questions to which our time is trying to find an answer. This book is an attempt to contribute to that answer.

PART I

The Life and Death of Civilizations

I

The Rise and Fall of Civilizations

SINCE the eighteenth century the habit has prevailed among Western historians to regard the history of humanity as one continuous development, an unbroken line, which in harmony with the spirit of the time was usually thought to be one of constant progress. In the study of history our Western society was taken as the point of departure from which historians worked backward, and as the end toward which all previous history had been developing. Historical events throughout the world and throughout the ages were, under the names of "Ancient History" and "Middle Ages," treated as a mere prologue to the history of Europe, which was the sea into which all the rivers of the past debouched. Just as in the concept of the universe before Copernicus the earth was automatically accepted as the center of the universe, so the linear concept of history construed the historical events of all times and peoples, whether they took place in China or Mexico, in the fourth century B.C. or the nineteenth century A.D., as part of one single coherent process leading up to the modern history of the Western world.

In the course of the last hundred years or so this self-centered view of history has been more and more abandoned under the impact of discoveries which laid bare the story of long-forgotten ages and brought evidence that the one-line concept does not tally with the facts of history.

On the one hand it is not correct that the history of mankind constitutes one continuous process of progress. We notice in history that certain areas during certain periods produce what is usually called civilization or culture. These civilizations are limited in time and in space, or, to say the least of it, there are periods and areas in which civilization thrives and others in which it is dormant. There was a civilization which originated in the Nile Valley, blossomed there, spread beyond the borders of that valley, but never reached, say, England or China or Peru. After a life span of about three thousand years it gradually petered out as a distinctive civilization with a character of its own and finally gave way to an era in that region which could not be called civilized any more. Similarly the civilization which originated in Rome and which had by the first century A.D. spread over the Mediterranean, the Middle East and Western Europe, subsequently disintegrated and was replaced by a Dark Age which lasted from about the fifth until the ninth century. Similar Dark Ages followed or preceded other civilizations.

This has led many modern historians to the conclusion that the development of civilization has not been one of uninterrupted progress: it has risen in certain regions in certain periods and then either temporarily fallen to rise again, or disappeared altogether.

At the same time the discoveries of modern times have brought ever stronger evidence that other societies in distant ages and countries have gone through experiences similar to our own.

Thus we have come to view Western civilization as one of many which have existed or exist, as we have come to consider the earth one of many planets revolving around the sun.

This does not necessarily imply a denial of progress. First of all, each civilization in itself shows one or more long ascending lines of progress. But even when a civilization disappears, valuable creations which it has produced in the way of technique, science, art, are inherited and used by a following civilization.

Thus our own civilization has heavily borrowed from ancient Greece and Rome in morality, philosophy, architecture, literature, government, law.

Finally each following civilization can, and in most cases has, brought forth a higher degree of control of the human and physical environment, and consequently a greater prosperity and greater spiritual or aesthetic achievements than its predecessor.

Nor does this view of civilizations degrade men or nations to inanimate tools in the hands of fate nor does it make human effort useless. History abounds with examples of nations and leaders which have by their determined will changed the course of history, stopped a process of decay or led a civilization to new greatness.

Since a certain similarity in the life course of different civilizations has been discovered, a clue to the future of our civilization has been sought by comparing it—or some of its aspects, such as its aesthetic or economic or political characteristics—to other civilizations and thus trying to discern what the future holds in store.

It is not the purpose of this book to review all these theories or pass judgment upon them. This has been done by others more competent for that undertaking. (As one of the latest examples the reader may be referred to Pitirim Sorokin's *Social Philosophies of an Age of Crisis,* a thorough and elaborate survey of many philosophies about the crisis of our time, to which we shall often have occasion to refer. That study differs from the present book in that the former is a scientific work for the expert student of philosophy and does not try to apply the conclusions of scientific investigation to our present civilization.) Also, such an attempt would swell this study to the size of an encyclopedia on the reader's bookshelf and to the weight of a stone in his literary stomach. Above all it would give this book a purpose different from the one it is intended to serve; it would become a comprehensive scientific work, written for the intellectual few. This is not what our time most needs. What it does need is faith in the historic task of our civilization and in its possibilities. It is to that faith that this work hopes to contribute. And if this undertaking is to bear any fruit, it must be kept within limits and expressed in language intelligible to the average citizen of the Western world.

*   *   *

Some of the comparative studies of civilization have limited themselves to the field of aesthetic forms, trying to establish analogies in the development of various arts within each civilization.

According to the British author Sir Flanders Petrie, for instance, there is a uniform sequence in which the different forms of art in each civilization emerge from the stage of archaism into that of free and rich expression. The sequence in which, according to him, they always come into bloom is, first, architecture and sculpture, then, in succession, painting, literature, music, mechanics, science, followed finally by what he calls wealth. According to the German author Paul Ligeti, however, the development of all civilizations has started with an "architectural stage," which implies order, effort, law, discipline and religion, and continued through a "plastic stage," which is a synthesis of the preceding and the subsequent stages, toward a "stage of painting," which stands for progress, freedom, mobility, disorder, materialism, utilitarianism, predominance of reason over faith.

Other authors have advanced theories which assert that within each civilization all forms of art pass through similar phases of birth, growth and decline, such as, for instance, an archaic, a classical and a decadent stage.

The limited value of all these theories attempting to establish similarities in the development of art in different cultures is summed up as follows in the judgment of one who, armed with extensive knowledge both of history and of the theories in this field, evaluated them as follows:

It can hardly be questioned that between the art systems of various cultures there exist many similarities in both small and great matters. . . .

Quite different, however, is the claim that the main stages of the life history of all art systems are the same, that there exists a uniform sequence of these stages, and that therefore the life curve of all art systems has practically the same configuration, with its zenith in the classic period and a decline in the direction of the initial (archaic) and the final (postclassic) periods. These claims appear to me to be questionable. There is a large body of material to support this doubt. [Sorokin, *op. cit.*, p. 40-41.]

When such rules are not overstated, however, they have a highly important cognitive value. To a considerable degree they make intelligible an otherwise incomprehensible jungle of chaotic historical events. . . . There is no doubt that several of the above generalizations are roughly valid, when they are not overextended beyond their legitimate boundary. [Sorokin, *op. cit.*, p. 45.]

Apart from these aesthetic philosophies of histories, limited in their scope to the artistic expressions of civilizations, many others have tried to evaluate the present crisis of our civilization against the wider background of history in all its aspects and the experiences of other civilizations. These philosophies have attracted the widest attention in our time because they strike at what people instinctively feel to be the heart of the matter: Does history hold a clue to the future of Western civilization?

For the reasons mentioned above we shall limit ourselves to those historical interpretations of the twentieth-century crisis of our civilization which seem most important, both on account of the value of their contents and on account of the influence they have exercised on the mind of our generation. We shall draw upon other works only where they are relevant to the general line of argument. Thus we shall in scientific fields covered by others make use of their work and rely on their conclusions as much as seems justified after critical scrutiny.

Once having in this way based ourselves upon a scientifically reliable platform, we shall try to assess the reality around us and scan the horizons of the future.

In practice this means that we shall first try to find certain characteristics of the rise and fall of civilizations (Part I); we shall then measure our present time by them (Part II), and finally draw the conclusions for the future of Western civilization (Part III).

II

A Russian View: Nikolai Danilevsky

THE idea that history repeats itself in the rise and fall of civilizations is by no means an invention of our time. The Stoics, Machiavelli, Montaigne and others held a similar idea, but none of them tried to test it thoroughly against the facts of history.

The first to elaborate slightly on this idea was the eighteenth-century Italian philosopher Giovanni Battista Vico who developed a theory of *ricorsi* (historical returns). Each nation, in his opinion, went through an identical cycle, rising from a "heroic age" of "barbarism of the senses," to a phase of true civilization, and relapsing in an overintellectual decadent "barbarism of reflection," after which the cycle of civilization closed —only to be succeeded by a new cycle, similar to the preceding, but with fresh cultural values added and therefore richer than its predecessor.

It was to take another hundred and fifty years before a more thorough comparison between different civilizations was drawn up. And even then it happened in an almost haphazard way, in the course of a study dealing with a different subject.

In 1869 Nikolai Danilevsky, a brilliant Russian government official who had produced studies on widely varied subjects, ranging from history to linguistics and from Darwinism to the devaluation of the Russian ruble, published in the magazine *Zaria* a series of articles entitled "Russia and Europe: a Viewpoint on the Political Relations between the Slavic and Germano-Romanic Worlds." In Russia the work immediately aroused great interest, but not until 1890 was a French translation published, and not until 1920 a German one. An English translation has never appeared, with the result that in the Anglo-Saxon world his ideas are even today little known. Yet they are of such wide scope and penetrating character that he may well be considered the spiritual forerunner of both his most famous successors in this field, Spengler and Toynbee—even though neither of the two pays any attention to him, probably because no translation in the language of either author existed at the moment of his writing.

The object of Danilevsky's treatise was, as its title indicates, not to draw up a comparative philosophy of civilizations; it was primarily to scrutinize the relations between Europe and Russia and to explain why these relations were inimical and were bound to remain so throughout the generations. This fact is ascribed by the author to an instinctive antipathy which Europe harbors against Russia, a country she considers alien to herself; this resentment in turn is traced to the circumstance that European civilization is on the decline, whereas that of Russia is in its ascendancy.

The picture which the author paints of the aggressiveness which Europe has shown toward Russia in the course of centuries and of the distrust with which it has consistently answered Russian sincerity is of even more interest today, if only for the insight it gives in the way the Slav mind views Europe. However, this part of Danilevsky's study is not directly relevant to the subject of this book and we can therefore confine ourselves to recommending its reading to all those who have to deal with Russia's relations with the West.

It is as a sideline to his sketch of this antagonism between

Europe and Russia that Danilevsky sets forth his theory about
the development of what he calls "historico-cultural types," but
which we shall merely indicate as "civilizations."

European civilization is by no means the universal civilization
—a thought new in those days—nor is it the only dynamic or
progressive one, says the Russian author; it is but one of many;
it covers only the area of the Germano-Romanic civilization.
Most other civilizations, including to a certain extent even the
Hellenic, originated outside Europe. So did the Russian, for Russia does not belong to Europe in the sense that it is a part or even
an offshoot of its civilization; it has taken almost no share in the
life and experiences of Europe, but has led an existence of its
own.

After thus having attacked and disposed of the self-centered-
ness which up to then characterized the Western view of history
and civilization, Danilevsky proceeds to develop his thesis: that
the total history of mankind is composed of a number of different
historical-cultural types, each of which has its own character and
its own contribution to make to the cultural treasury of mankind.
Danilevsky distinguishes twelve such civilizations, which are, in
chronological order: the Egyptian, the Chinese, the Assyro-
Babylonian, the Phoenician-Chaldean or Ancient-Semitic, the
Hindu, the Iranian, the Hebrew, the Greek, the Roman, the Neo-
Semitic or Arabian, and the Germano-Romanic or European;
and in the Western Hemisphere: the Mexican and the Peruvian,
which both met violent death without completing their life course.

Danilevsky divides all human tribes and peoples into three
groups, according to the part they play with regard to civilization.
The first group comprises those who constitute positive, i.e., creative forces by bringing forth the civilizations enumerated above.
The second group comprises the peoples which play a negative
or destructive role, such as the Mongols, the Huns and the Turks
in earlier times. The third group comprises those populations
which neither reach the level of civilizations, nor act as the de-

stroyer of decaying civilizations; they constitute the amorphous masses which do not make history either in the positive or negative way, but are used by the positive or negative historical forces as passive material for their activity and achievement.

Besides the positive cultural types of civilizations there are in the human universe intermittent temporary agencies like the Huns, the Mongols, and the Turks who, having performed their destructive mission, have helped dying civilizations to die and then scattering their remains, return to their previous nothingness and disappear. We can call them the *negative agencies* of history. Sometimes, however, constructive as well as destructive missions are performed by the same tribe, as for instance, by the Germans and the Arabs. Finally, there are tribes or peoples whose creative *élan* is, for some reason, *arrested* at an early stage and who are therefore destined to be neither constructive nor destructive, neither positive nor negative agencies of history. They present only *ethnographic material*, a sort of inorganic matter entering the historical organisms, the historico-cultural types. Undoubtedly these tribes increase the variety and richness of the historical types, but in *themselves* they do not achieve any historical individuality.

Sometimes the dead and decayed civilizations disintegrate to the level of this ethnographic material until a new formative (creative) principle unites their elements with a mixture of other elements into a new historical organism, until this principle calls them to an independent historical life in the form of a new historico-cultural type. The peoples that made up the Western Roman Empire serve as an example of this. They became ethnographic material after the disintegration of the Empire and re-emerged in a new form, known as the Romanic peoples, after experiencing the influence of the Germanic formative principle.

To sum up: The historical role of a tribe or people is three-fold: it is either the positive creative role of a historico-cultural type (civilization), or the destructive role—the so-called scourges of God that render the *coup de grâce* to senile, agonizing civilizations, or the role of serving the purposes of others as ethnographic material. [*Zaria*, No. 2, pp. 89-91.]

Danilevsky then proceeds to formulate five general laws or similarities which apply to all peoples in comparable phases of development.

The fourth of these laws, which stresses the necessity of diversity and independence of the "ethnographic material" of a civilization, is of great importance in our present day, and may become still more so in the future. We shall have reason to return to it in the latter part of this book. What is of interest here is that in connection with this law Danilevsky, writing three quarters of a century before Toynbee, established the principle that *a civilization is the real unit of historical study*. In ancient Greece a special history of Athens or Sparta is impossible outside the context of Greek civilization; similarly in Europe the histories of France, Germany, Italy cannot be studied outside the context of European civilization. On the other hand countries not within the same civilization have little in common and their histories are therefore almost independent of each other.

With regard to the subject of this book more important still is Danilevsky's fifth law:

> The course of development of historico-cultural types is similar to the life-course of these perennials whose period of growth lasts indefinitely, but whose period of blossoming and fruitbearing is relatively short and exhausts them once and for all. [*Zaria*, No. 3, p. 2.]

In elaborating this law the author contends that a culture-historical type usually passes through three phases of development (*Zaria*, No. 3, p. 27).

The first or ancient phase is the "stage of ethnographic material," which may last for millennia and ends with the transmutation of the purely ethnographic form of living into an organized society.

The second or middle stage covers the process of building cultural and political independence; this is the phase of the accumulation and organization of creative forces for the next phase.

The latter is called by the author the "stage of civilization"; in this period the culture-historical type reaches the full bloom of its creative productivity and the materialization of its ideals of individual and social well-being. This phase is comparatively short—about four to six centuries—because its creative activity is a drain on its forces and no civilization "is endowed with the privilege of endless progress, and since every people is eventually worn out and exhausted creatively."

Consequently this blossoming is inevitably followed by a decline and disintegration of the civilization, which might—although Danilevsky does not do so—be termed a fourth stage. This process of disintegration, like many processes in nature, sets in well before its outward phenomena become noticeable. Just as summer reaches its greatest heat after the days have started to shorten again, and the highest temperatures of the day occur after the sun has passed its zenith, and the highest point in a man's life occurs in his middle age after the period of his greatest productive capacity has ended, so the decay of a civilization sets in when it is still blooming and appears to be at its zenith. The author even alleges, with particular reference to Europe, that the weaker the creative force becomes, the stronger the desire for expansion and world domination grows.

The degeneration shows itself either in a state of apathy, petrifaction and self-satisfaction, in which the forms of the past are endlessly copied as a petrified ideal, or in a period of political and social contradictions renting the body and soul social, a period of conflicts and despair. This period usually in the end also reverts to the state of "apathy of petrifaction."

These are the main characteristics of Danilevsky's general philosophy in so far as they pertain to our study. As will become clear in the next few chapters, nearly every one of them constitutes the germ of an idea which has later on been enlarged by Spengler or, more often, by Toynbee. The resemblances are all the more striking since neither of these two has been aware of Danilevsky's ideas, and since Danilevsky did not consider himself European and was therefore writing from the viewpoint of a different civilization.

On the basis of the ideas summarized above Danilevsky arrived at his explanation of the inherent hostility between European and Slavic-Russian civilization. The former is about five hundred years older than the latter, which is only now passing from its second phase into that of its "civilization" or bloom, whereas the former has reached the end of that period. Its decline, according to Danilevsky, started as early as the seventeenth century, but only became visible in the nineteenth; it is apparent in a weakening of creativity and in a decline of Christian faith, accompanied by an increasing cynicism and desire for world domination in the political and economic as well as in the cultural fields. Because of Europe's desire to impose its own culture on the whole world, no friendship is possible between it and the youthful Russian civilization, whose historic mission it is to check Europe's lust for domination. Once Europe has settled its internal affairs, Danilevsky says, war between it and united Slavdom is inevitable. In this clash Slavdom will emerge as victor over senile and exhausted Europe and will take over its role of world leadership.

Today these tones sound more familiar than at the time when they were written. They well justify the appreciation given by a present-day Russian-born philosopher:

> Begun as a pamphlet of the highest grade, it demonstrated its political contentions to such a degree that it became a brilliant treatise on the philosophy of history and cultural sociology, and ended up by being an unusually shrewd and essentially correct piece of political prognostication and prophecy. In reading its political sections, one cannot fail to see a remarkable similarity between Danilevsky's views on the Russo-European relationships and prospects, and those of the Soviet government on this same subject. If one removes the Marxist terminology and a few other insignificant details from the policies and political propaganda of the Soviet government, Danilevsky's and the Soviet leaders' ideologies regarding Russo-European relations are essentially similar. [Sorokin. *op. cit.*, p. 71.]

III

Oswald Spengler's View of
Civilizations

OSWALD SPENGLER was a remarkable character. In his
oddly shaped head, which looked like an egg befathered
by a billiard ball, he conceived a theory about the life and death
of civilizations which has had a tremendous influence on modern
thinking in this meeting ground of philosophy and history.

Spengler's book *The Decline of the West*, conceived before,
written during and published after World War I, made a deep
impression in the early twenties on a Europe trembling with
exhaustion and deeply shaken in its innate sense of superiority as
the natural leader of the world and the source of all intellect,
industrial production and capital. For the same reasons after
World War II a revival of interest in Spengler's work was noticeable in a number of new studies and reprintings both in Germany
and the United States. Even so, in Europe, where his name has
a resounding reputation and many are in danger of falling prey
to the paralyzing idea of the decline of the West, few have read
the book or are familiar with its main line of thought, whereas
in the Americas he is still less known to the general public.

To whoever has taken the trouble to struggle through the two
heavy volumes of the work this is not surprising. It is more
surprising that sufficient people have trudged through these
sands to create a certain response. Any scientific work on such
a subject is bound to be hard reading, but in this case the reading is rendered trebly difficult by two additional circumstances.

17

Quite apart from the subject, the style is, even for a German scientific book, heavy and cumbersome. In addition, its involved subject matter is still further complicated by ingredients which spring from the author's personal outlook on life, but which are entirely foreign to the subject. For Oswald Spengler was a Prussian and a militarist if ever there was one. The preconceived ideas which speak with uncompromising violence from almost every page of his book bear witness to this attitude toward life. This is an additional reason why to the average reader in a democratic country his book may easily seem unconvincing and even repulsive. This unfortunately has tended to shroud from the general public in many, and particularly in the English-speaking countries, the wealth of valuable facts and thought contained in his work. If however, one tries to sieve facts from interpretation, one sees emerging from those heavy volumes a picture of two different Spenglers: one is Spengler the autocrat, the militarist, the forerunner of National Socialism; the other is Spengler the scientist, the thinker, the philosopher, the visionary; one is the spiritual father of Hitler, the other the spiritual son of Goethe. This dual and conflicting personality must have made itself constantly felt in Spengler's soul, as it does, indeed, in the soul of the whole German nation; it can be felt in the vehemence with which he rejects such "soft" notions as impartiality, morality, idealism, philosophy. Only a man who is afraid of being influenced by such notions would reject them with such uncontrolled violence.

The impartial student who tries to distinguish as clearly as possible between these two sides of Spengler's work finds that they can be separated to a large extent. The general similarity in the development of different civilizations which he tries to establish can be accepted without accepting the appreciative or deprecating estimate which Spengler puts on their different phases and without accepting all the examples he uses or all the extremes to which he tries to push his system.

In order to try and separate these two aspects we shall in the next chapter point out a number of fundamental conceptions on which Spengler's personal appraisal of times, facts and persons is based, and which can only be considered as unacceptable prejudices from the point of view of a civilization which has its roots in Christianity and the freedom of man.

Yet when the fringe of these prejudices is taken away, the impressive frame of Spengler's comparison of civilizations still remains intact.

What is this framework?

THE ESSENCE OF SPENGLER'S PHILOSOPHY OF CIVILIZATIONS

Reduced to its simplest form it is this:

Like all forces in nature, civilizations follow a common pattern of birth, growth, decay and death. Hence it is possible to draw a parallel between the life course of different civilizations, and to compare the consecutive stages of each civilization as expressed in the forms of their politics, economics, religion, art, science and other aspects of organized society. Spengler draws these comparisons in hundreds of examples, with effects which are sometimes astonishing and sometimes verge on the ridiculous. Thus he builds up his "morphology of cultures," a science of the life and death of civilizations.

This science, if Spengler's fundamental thesis is correct, not only enables us to draw comparisons between past stages of civilizations, but also to predict the future course of our own civilization. This is what Spengler did and what created such a deep impression in our Western world. In order to be able to judge his conclusions, we must first look at the general pattern of civilizations as sketched by the master hand of Spengler.

Following the example set by Goethe in his essay "*Geistesepochen,*" Spengler distinguishes four consecutive phases of a culture: its preliminary, early, late and civilized stages. Spengler, however, uses the word "culture" exclusively for the "early" and "late" stages, i.e., those of bloom and of fruition; the word "civilization" he reserves for the last phase, that of sterility and petrification. A culture in his terminology is what most authors would call "a living civilization"; a "civilization" in his terminology is what others might call "a dying civilization."

The birth of a culture is preceded by a "precultural period," an interval, either in time or space, between two cultures. In this period men are born, live, love, work and die, as always, but in it the organization of society does not take such an organized form, nor produce a religion, art or science of sufficient importance as to constitute a "culture." It is a *historyless* society in the sense of Spengler's words; which means that it contains no events of importance to the development of civilization, although it no doubt does contain events which are important to the contemporaries.

With regard to our Western civilization this precultural period is represented by the Merovingian-Carolingian Era (approximately from A.D. 500-900), with regard to the classical civilization by the Mycenean Age (1600-1100 B.C.).

The birth of a "culture" becomes apparent by the appearance of a strong, simple style in the field of arts, science or religion, such as the Doric style in the classical and the Gothic style in the Western culture. It is usually accompanied by the birth of a myth of grand style, such as the Vedic religion in India, the Homeric epics in Greece and the medieval German myths (Edda, Nibelungenlied) in Europe. Judging by these symptoms the birth of the classical culture can be put at about 1100 B.C., that of the Western culture at about A.D. 900.

The first or early period of the culture is characterized in the political field by feudalism. The soil is the main source of production, hence the countryside, and its owner and ruler, the feudal nobleman, dominate the political field. In the spiritual field this gives birth to a chivalric-religious idealism. The economy of this period is mainly agrarian; the "city" is as yet not more than a market or stronghold. Struggles of the vassals between themselves and against the overlord gradually bring about disintegration of the feudal system and lead to aristocratic states and the birth of cities, which brings the first period to an end. In China this phase is represented by the early Chou period (1300-800 B.C.), in Europe by the era of the German-Roman Empire, the Crusades and the struggle between Empire and Papacy (Gothic period, A.D. 900-1500).

With the birth and rise of the cities starts a new phase, the "late period of culture." In Greece this is the Ionic period (650-300 B.C.), characterized by the blossoming of the city-state, culminating in the Golden Age of Pericles; in Rome it encompasses the replacement of the rule of the Etruscan kings by that of the patricians, followed by the struggle between patricians and plebeians. In Western civilization it is the period of the Baroque (1500-1800). Yet its origin must be traced back to the Renaissance towns in Italy and France and the Hansa towns in Northwestern Europe; it is brought to a close by the final victory of the third estate in the French revolution. In China it is the late Chou period (800-500 B.C.), which finds its visible end in the fall of the Chou dynasty in 441 B.C., an event comparable to the French revolution.

The earmark of this "late" period is the bloom and preponderance of the towns. None has demonstrated as clearly as Spengler that "world-history is city-history."

It is a conclusive fact that all great Cultures are town-cultures. Higher man of the Second Age is a town-tied animal. Here is the real criterion of "world-history" that differentiates it with utter sharpness from man's history—*world-history is the history of the civic man.* Peoples, states, politics, religion, all arts, and all sciences rest upon *one* prime phenomenon of human being: the town.

But the real miracle is the birth of the *soul* of a town . . . . What distinguishes a town from a village is not size, but the presence of a soul. [Vol. II, Ch. IV (A), pp. 90-91.]

The towns bring forth the bourgeoisie, which politically, economically and spiritually, gradually takes over the power and leadership from the two original classes of each culture, feudal nobility and priesthood. In the field of art and science this period gives birth to a number of urban and conscious arts in the hands of gifted individuals: it is the "period of the Great Masters," as exemplified by the great sculptors and architects and philosophers of the fifth century in Greece, the great painters of the Italian and Dutch schools, the great German composers, the Reformers and Humanists, followed by the English Rationalists in the seventeenth and the French Encyclopedists in the eighteenth century. In the city

being becomes more and more languid, sensation and reason more and more powerful. Man becomes intellect, "free" like the nomads, whom he comes to resemble, but narrower and colder than they. All art, all religion and science, become slowly intellectualized, alien to the land, incomprehensible to the peasant of the soil.

In the economic system and economic conceptions of the cities, too, money becomes an independent power, cut from its links with the soil. The whole process—in brief—culminates in the victory of the town over the countryside, of money over landed property, of the intelligentsia over tradition, of the masses over the privileged castes.

We then finally enter upon the phase which Spengler describes as "civilization," the consummation of each culture, its final, but least creative period. This period is the most important from our point of view because our civilization has, according to Spengler, entered into it with Napoleon.

Politically this phase can be subdivided into two clearly separate periods. The first can best be characterized by the name it bears in Chinese history: the Period of the Contending States, of which Spengler says:

The period 480-230 B.C. is called by the Chinese historians the "Period of the Contending States"; it culminated in a century of unbroken war-

fare between mass-armies with frightful social upheavals, and out of it
came the "Roman" state of Chin as founder of a Chinese Imperium.
This phase Egypt experienced between 1780 and 1580, of which the
last century was the "Hyksos" time. The Classical experienced it from
Chaeronea (338), and, at the high pitch of horror, from the Gracchi
(133) to Actium (31 B.C.). And it is the destiny of the West-European-
American world for the nineteenth and twentieth centuries.

During this period the center of gravity changes, as from Attica to
Latium, so from the Hwang-ho (at Ho-nan-fu) to the Yang-tse (modern
province of Hupei). [Vol. II, Ch. II, Section V, p. 40-41.]

The author could at the moment of his writing not yet add,
although he must prophetically have foreseen, that thirty years
later the center of gravity of the Western world, too, would have
shifted (across the Atlantic).

The "period of the contending states," which usually lasts
about two centuries, is terminated by the final victory of one of
the contending powers whose authority consequently stretches
in one form or another over the whole region to which civilization has then spread: the "imperial state" is born, and with it
the last phase of civilization. During this period the whole
civilized world is ruled directly or indirectly, officially or un-
officially, *de jure* or *de facto* from one central spot by one almost
omnipotent leader, whether his title be Caesar, Emperor, Mogul
or something else. Great "international" wars, that is wars between what used to be the states within the empire, no longer take
place, so that one can justly speak of an era of world peace, of
Pax Romana. The place of these wars is taken, on the one hand
by smaller struggles along the frontiers to hold at bay the
"barbarians" outside the empire, and on the other hand by internal struggles for the throne, which may take the form of
"private wars," palace revolutions, *coups d'état* or similar results of rivalries between persons, cliques or factions.

This last phase, this "winter" of each civilization, for which
Spengler uses the word "civilization" by exclusion of the previous
phases, thus is politically made up of a period of great wars

followed by a period of civilization-wide peace. In addition to the main trends mentioned, Spengler elaborately describes the following phenomena as distinctive of this phase of world peace.

SPENGLER'S CHARACTERISTICS OF THE LAST PHASE OF
CIVILIZATION

a. World Peace and Caesarism

Since the whole area of the civilization is under the control of one power and ultimately of one man, there are no longer any "national wars." This, however, by no means implies the end of bloodshed. The "national wars" are merely replaced by "private wars" the stake of which is the personal power in the universal state or part of it: this is the period of the Caesars, the strong individuals, the dictators, the military rulers, the period of Vikingism.

These rulers start to appear in the period of the contending states, but they get their full opportunity when the phase of world peace has set in: when the nations have abandoned their will to power, that of the private individuals takes its place.

With world-peace—the peace of high policies—the "sword-side" of history retreats, and the "spindle-side" rules again. Henceforth there are only *private* histories, private destinies, private ambitions, from top to bottom—from the miserable troubles of fellaheen, to the dreary feuds of Caesars for the private possession of the world.

The wars of the age of world-peace are private wars, more fearful than any State wars because they are formless. For world-peace—which has often existed in fact—involves the private renunciation of war on the part of the immense majority. But along with this it involves an unavowed readiness to submit to being booty of others who do *not* renounce it.

On this *spiritual* premise a second Vikingism develops. The state of being "in form" passes from nations to bands and retinues of adventurers, self-styled Caesars, seceding generals, barbarian Kings, and what not. [Vol. II, Ch. XI, Section X, p. 434-435.]

World-peace is always a one-sided resolve. The *Pax Romana* had for the later soldier-emperors and Germanic band-kings only the one practical significance that it made a formless population of a hundred millions a mere object for the will-to-power of small warrior-groups. This peace costs the peaceful sacrifices beside which the losses of Cannae seem vanishingly small. The Babylonian, Chinese, Indian, Egyptian worlds pass from one conqueror's hand to another and it is their own blood that pays for the contest. That is their peace.

A resolute leader who collects ten thousand adventurers about him can do as he pleases. [Vol. II, Ch. VI, V, p. 186.]

b. The World-city

None has as well as Spengler foreseen the rise, none has as eloquently described the charms and strangling clutch of that alluring and petrifying monster, the "megalopolis," which with its lethal beauty and irresistible attraction blossoms forth at the end of each civilization.

Finally, there arises the monstrous symbol and vessel of the completely emancipated intellect, the world-city, the centre in which the course of a world-history ends by winding itself up. A handful of gigantic places in each Civilization disfranchises and disvalues the entire motherland of its own Culture under the contemptuous name of "the provinces." The "provinces" are now everything whatsoever—land, town *and* city— except those two or three points. There are no longer noblesse and bourgeoisie, freemen and slaves, Hellenes and Barbarians, believers and unbelievers, *but only cosmopolitans and provincials.* [Vol. II, Chapter IV, IV, pp. 98-99.]

The world-city breeds a human type which is another characteristic of the last period of each culture:

c. The Intellectual Nomad

So long as the hearth has a pious meaning as the actual and genuine centre of a family, the old relation to the land is not wholly extinct. But when *that* too, follows the rest into oblivion, and the mass of tenants and bed-occupiers in the sea of houses leads a vagrant existence from shelter to shelter like the hunters and pastors of the "pre" time, then the intellectual nomad is completely developed. [Vol. II, Ch. IV, V, p. 100.]

And another note of striking actuality for our present day is added: "Diodorus tells us of a deposed Egyptian King who was reduced to living in one of these wretched upper-floor tenements of Rome."

Long, long ago the country bore the country-town and nourished it with her best blood. Now the giant city sucks the country dry, insatiably and incessantly demanding and devouring fresh streams of men, till it wearies and dies in the midst of an almost uninhabited waste of country. Once the full sinful beauty of this last marvel of all history has captured a victim, it never lets him go. Primitive folk can loose themselves from the soil and wander, but the intellectual nomad never. Homesickness for the great city is keener than any other nostalgia. Home is for him any one of these giant cities but even the nearest village is alien territory. He would sooner die upon the pavements than go "back" to the land. [*Ibid*, p. 102.]

d. Declining Birthrate

An accompanying phenomenon of the era of the world-cities is a gradual leveling off of the increase of the population, followed by a stagnation and finally a process of depopulation which may last for centuries. The sterility of civilized man puts an end to the drama of civilization.

This phenomenon, according to Spengler, is "a metaphysical turn towards death." Man, as a race, no longer *wants* to live. Life itself has become questionable.

When the ordinary thought of a highly cultivated people begins to regard "having children" as a question of "pro's and con's," the great turning point has come. . . .

When reasons have to be put forward at all in a question of life, life itself has become questionable. At that point begins prudent limitation of the number of births. In the classical world the practice was deplored by Polybius as the ruin of Greece, and yet even at his date it had long been established in the great cities; in subsequent Roman times it became appallingly general. At first explained by the economic misery of the times, very soon it ceased to explain itself at all. [*Ibid*. p. 104.]

As a result of this development we find that at the end of each civilization the world-cities, like the provincial towns at an earlier stage, become depopulated, and are finally only inhabited by small groups using their stone masses as shelter like primitive men in the Stone Age.

Pataliputra, Asoka's capital, was an immense and completely uninhabited waste of houses when the Chinese traveller Hiouen-tsang visited it about A.D. 635. . . .

In a long series of Classical writers from Polybius onward we read of old renowned cities in which the streets have become lines of empty, crumbling shells, where the cattle browse in forum and gymnasium, and the amphitheatre is a sown field, dotted with emergent statues and herbs. Rome had in the fifth century of our era the population of a village, but its imperial palaces were still habitable. [*Ibid.* p. 107.]

e. Preponderance, Followed by Decline of Money

With the rise of the towns, followed by preponderance of the world-city, the disappearance of all bonds with the soil and the hegemony of intellectualism, money reaches the zenith of its power. Created originally as a *measure* of values, that is of the things that had real value at the time, such as land, cattle, houses, slaves, the link with those original values becomes weaker with the growth of the cities and the intricacy of the economic system, until finally money comes to be considered as a value in itself, more desirable than those things of which it was originally only designated to measure the value.

Gold is no longer measured against the cow, but the cow against the gold. [*Ibid.* p. 483.]

Yet, in the Imperial Age the power of money is finally defeated by the powers of blood and sword.

The coming of Caesarism breaks the dictature of money and its political weapon democracy. After a long triumph of world-city economy and its interests over political creative force, the political side of life manifests itself after all as the stronger of the two. The sword is victorious over **the** money, the master-will subdues again the plunderer-will. [Vol. II, Ch. XIV, III, p. 506.]

f. Disappearance of Creativeness

In the last phase of civilization the creative spirit has disappeared; the civilization has reached its finished form. No new great creations appear, either in art, or in religion or in politics. Life has become intellectualized and commercialized, and although science may flourish, and there may be much talk and time and money spent on art or religion, it has lost its creative drive. The forms have ultimately been established; many changes, variations and mixtures between them may still appear, but no fundamentally *new* forms appear any more. All great problems have been solved; the struggles that go on are no longer, as in the "culture" phase, about ideas, but purely for power.

In the history, the genuine history, of higher men the stake fought for and the basis of the animal struggle to prevail is ever the actualization of something that is essentially spiritual, the translation of an idea into a living historical form. This applies equally to the struggle of big style-tendencies in art (Gothic and Renaissance), of philosophy (Stoics and Epicurians), of political ideals (Oligarchy and Tyrannis), and of economic forms (Capitalism and Socialism). But the post-history is void of all this. All that remains is the struggle for mere power, for animal advantage per se. Whereas previously power was always serving the Idea somehow or other, in the late Civilization even the most convincing illusion of an idea is only the mask for purely zoological strivings. [Vol. II, Ch. II, VI, p. 49.]

Once the Imperial Age has arrived, there are no more political problems. People manage with the situation as it is and the powers that be. In the period of Contending States, torrents of blood had reddened the pavements of all world-cities, so that the great truths of Democracy might be turned into actualities, and for the winning of rights without which life seemed not worth the living. Now these rights are won, but the grandchildren cannot be moved even by punishment to make use of them. A hundred years more, and even the historians will no longer understand the old controversies. Already by Caesar's time reputable people had almost ceased to take part in the elections. [Vol. II, Ch. XII, X, p. 432.]

This lack of creativeness, according to Spengler, is characteristic of our time, which forms part of what in his terminology is a "civilization" period; our time is comparable not to Pericles' Athens, but to Caesar's Rome.

What is practised as art to-day is impotence and falsehood. Look where one will, can one find the great personalities that would justify the claim that there is still an art of determinate necessity? Look where one will, can one find the self-evidently necessary task that awaits such an artist?

We go through all the exhibitions, the concerts, the theatres and find only industrious cobblers and noisy fools, who delight to produce something for the market, something that will "catch on" with a public for whom art and music and drama have long ceased to be spiritual necessities. [Vol. I, Ch. VIII, IX, p. 293.]

The same applied to Alexandria and Rome:

Alexandria, too, had problem-dramatists and box-office artists whom it preferred to Sophocles, and painters who invented new tendencies and successfully bluffed their public.

All the Roman portrait statues, male and female, go back for posture and mien to a very few Hellenic types; these, copied more or less true to style, served for torsos, while the heads were executed as "likenesses" by simple craftsmen who possessed the knack. . . . For 1500 years (Amasis I to Cleopatra) Egypticism piled portrait on portrait in the same way. . . . So it has been in the last Act of all Cultures. [*Ibid.* p. 295.]

g. The Second Religiousness

One of the final phenomena of each civilization is what Spengler calls the "second religiousness," a return in somewhat changed forms of the religious feeling of the springtime. In order to understand this movement it is necessary to remember the development through which spiritual life in the civilization has by that time progressed.

In the springtime religious feeling blossoms with all the strength and simplicity of its primitive force. When the church tends to become too rigid and stray away from the original meaning of the faith, a reformation attempts to bring it back. This is followed by a period of puritanism, a fanatic revival of piety, which often tries to impose its religion through politics and force upon others: Pythagoras, Mohammed, Cromwell.

In puritanism lies already the hidden seed of rationalism, which appears in each late period: Confucius and Buddha, Socrates and Rousseau. In its wake follows materialism.

Spengler summarizes this development in the following sentences:

Culture is ever synonymous with religious creativeness. Every great Culture begins with a mighty theme that rises out of the pre-urban country-side, is carried through in the cities of art and intellect, and closes with a finale of materialism in the world-cities.

As a reaction to this extreme rationalism, this intellectualism, there start to appear moods of myth, of enjoying the charm of the irrational, the unnatural, the repulsive, and even, if need be, the merely silly: the Serapis cult in Alexandria, Isis cult in Republican Rome, Chaldean astrology. These are fashions, a form of relaxation, a "let's pretend"; they are the "isms" in our time. These show the need of, and are a prelude to, the "second religiousness" which appears in all fully formed civilizations, as "the necessary counterpart of Caesarism, which is the final political constitution of Late Civilizations."

Every "Age of Enlightenment" proceeds from an unlimited optimism of the reason—always associated with the type of the megalopolitan— to an equally unqualified scepticism. . . . With this the possibilities of physics as a critical mode of world-understanding are exhausted, and the hunger for metaphysics presents itself afresh. [Vol. II, Ch. IX, VI, p. 311.]

The second religiousness is not born in the upper classes, but in the masses. Specimens are: the myth of Pan-Ku in China after 200 B.C., and the Vishnu and Shiwa doctrines in India at about

300 B.C. Furthermore Caesarism itself, in the Chinese as in the Roman Empire, gave birth to an emperor cult.

Finally, second religiousness ends up in the fellah religions and becomes historyless again; opposition between cosmopolitan and provincial piety vanishes. Centuries pass unimportantly. New forms of the old religions appear, change, intergrow, as for instance the composite of Buddhism, Confucianism and Taoism that constitutes the religion of China, or the Islam of the present-day East.

Western civilization, according to Spengler, is still many generations short of its second religiousness, which according to his theory should take the form of a return to Gothic Christianity.

THE END OF CIVILIZATION—THE RETURN TO HISTORYLESS SOCIETY

With the disappearance of creativeness, both physical and spiritual civilization finally disintegrates and collapses. In one of his most moving passages, Spengler describes the society which prevails after that.

With the formed state, high history also lays itself down wearily to sleep. Man becomes a plant again, adhering to the soil, dumb and enduring. The timeless village and the "eternal" peasant reappear, begetting children and burying seed in Mother-Earth—a busy, not inadequate swarm, over which the tempest of soldier-emperors passingly blows. In the midst of the land lie the old world-cities, empty receptacles of an extinguished soul in which a historyless mankind slowly nests itself. Men live from hand to mouth, with petty thrifts and petty fortunes, and endure. Masses are trampled on in the conflicts of the conquerors who contend for the power and the spoil of this world, but the survivors fill up the gaps with a primitive fertility and suffer on. And while in high places there is eternal alternance of victory and defeat, those in the depths pray, pray with the mighty piety of the Second Religiousness that has overcome all doubts for ever. There, in the souls, world-peace, the peace of God, the bliss of grey-haired monks and hermits, is become actual—and there alone. It has awakened that depth in the endurance of suffering which the historical man in the thousand years of his developments has never known. Only with the end of grand History does holy still Being reappear. It is a drama noble in its aimlessness, noble and aimless as the course of the stars, the rotation of the earth, and alternance of land and sea, of ice and virgin forest upon its face. We may marvel at it or we may lament it—but it is there. [Vol. II, Ch. XI, X, p. 435.]

THE PRESENT STAGE OF WESTERN CIVILIZATION

For Western civilization the "late period of culture," the era of the supremacy of the town and of the bourgeoisie, has passed, according to Spengler. The bourgeoisie, the third estate, won its final victory with the French Revolution. Hence the nineteenth century has seen the high tide of democracy, parliamentarism, intellect, money which has since then been on the wane, consciously or unconsciously, perceived or unperceived.

Today Parliamentarism is in full decay. . . .
With the beginning of the twentieth century Parliamentarianism (even English) is tending rapidly towards taking up itself the role that it once assigned to the kingship: It is becoming an impressive spectacle for the multitude of the Orthodox, while the center of gravity of big policy, already *de jure* transferred from the Crown to the People's representatives, is passing *de facto* from the latter to unofficial groups and the will of unofficial personages. [Vol. II, Ch. XI, VII, p. 415-416.]

With this enters the age of gigantic conflicts, in which we find ourselves to-day. It is the transition from Napoleonism to Caesarism, a general phase of evolution, which occupies at least two centuries and can be shown to exist in all Culture. [*Ibid.*]

For us this time of Contending States began with Napoleon and his violent-arbitrary government by order. His head was the first in our world to make effective the notion of a military and at the same time popular world-domination. . . . If the nineteenth century has been relatively poor in great wars—and revolutions—and has overcome its worst crises diplomatically by means of congresses, this has been due precisely to the continuous and terrific war-preparedness which has made disputants, fearful at the eleventh hour of the consequences, postpone the definitive decision again and again, and led to the substitution of chess-moves for war. . . . But this second century (i.e. the twentieth) will be one of *actually* Centending States. *These* armies are not substitutes for war—they are *for* war, and they *want* war. Within two generations it will be they whose will prevails over that of all the comfortables put together. In these wars of theirs for the heritage of the whole world, continents will be staked; India, China, South-Africa, Russia, Islam called out, new technics and tactics played and counterplayed. The great cosmopolitan foci of power will dispose at their pleasure of smaller states— their territory, their economy and their men alike—all that is now merely province, passive object, means to end, and its destinies are without importance to the great march of things. . . .

Again and again between these catastrophes of blood and terror the cry rises up for re-conciliation of the peoples and for peace on earth. [Vol. II, Ch. XI, IX, p. 429.]

For a book conceived before, and written during the First World War some of these prophesies seem to have been uncomfortably accurate. The same applies to Spengler's description of the character of the wars in the period of the contending states.

In every Culture, the technique of war hesitatingly followed the advance of craftsmanship, until at the beginning of the Civilization it suddenly takes the lead, presses all mechanical possibilities of the time relentlessly into its service, and under pressure of military necessity even opens up new domains hitherto unexploited. [Vol. II, Ch. XI, VIII, p. 420.]

The wars of this period, according to Spengler, are no longer wars limited to relatively small armies and until one of the parties declares himself exhausted; they are wars of gigantic armies, aimed at, and continued until the annihilation of the opponent. They are, in a modern word, *total wars*.

In this setting our place and the part we are to play in Western culture is, according to Spengler, inexorably determined by destiny. This is the gloomy message he lays down in the closing sentences of his book:

For us, whom a Destiny has placed in this Culture, and at this moment of its development—the moment when money is celebrating its last victories, and the Caesarism that is to succeed approaches with quiet, firm step—our direction, willed and obligatory at once, is set for us within narrow limits, and on any other terms life is not worth the living. We have not the freedom to reach to this or to that, but the freedom to do the necessary or to do nothing. And a task that historic necessity has set *will* be accomplished with the individual or against him. [Vol. II, Ch. XIV, III, p. 507.]

IV

Spengler the Militarist—and the Visionary

IN THE preceding chapter we have tried to give an outline of Spengler's philosophy about the life and death of civilizations. Unfortunately in Spengler's book the general lines of this majestic structure are almost hidden from the reader's view by a mass of loud prejudices plastered along its façade, like a building in the center of a modern city the architectural design of which is lost behind a screen of neon signs.

It is important to throw the spotlight on these violent prejudices and brand them for what they are, because not only do they threaten to shroud his concept of civilizations, but also they strongly influence his evaluation of our present time and his conclusions about the fate of our civilization. Here then, follow the main characteristics of Spengler's appreciation of values, expressed, where possible, in his own words.

SPENGLER'S PREJUDICES

Undemocratic Concept of Society

Spengler's view of society—society in *any* phase of development of a civilization—is essentially undemocratic. The fundamental principle of democracy that all men are born equal and are entitled to equal rights, is entirely alien to him. In his view every country, every nation, whether formally ruled by a monarch or dictator, by an oligarchy, or by a parliament is *in fact* ruled by a small minority driven by a strong will-to-power, an "aristocracy" in the original sense of the word: government by the best. Hence in his idea citizens are always and in every society inevitably divided into *subjects* and *objects* of government, the ruling minority and the ruled mass.

"The life-unit—even in the case of the animals—is subdivided into subjects and objects of government" (Vol. II, Ch. XII, p. 441.)

Spengler is not entirely blind to the value of the democratic system and the democratic era, but he is unable to see it as anything more than a passing phase in each culture. Of democracy's fundamental value or truth he is obviously by no means convinced. In keeping with his allegedly objective rendering of historic facts he does not express any opinion upon the "justness" or "rightness" of a particular form of government; yet the reader cannot escape the impression that Spengler's personal preference goes to the caste system, and is averse to democracy. Hence he is unable to perceive democracy as anything but the form in which a new class, the bourgeoisie, with its inherent powers of money and intellect, cloaks its will-to-power and its rule over the passive mass, which is a free electorate in name only.

Spengler thus commits the error which in the end has been fatal to all authoritarian rulers of history.

While it is of course true that every nation in the world is in practice governed and run by a small minority, Spengler overlooked the fact that this minority, whether it be composed of court, priesthood, feudal nobility, urban patriciate, or parliamentary and labor leaders, cannot allow itself with impunity to overstep certain boundaries of what is felt by the masses to be just and fair. At all times, in all nations, the masses have in the end revolted against what they considered unjust or cruel or unholy or highly inefficient administration. This proves that the ruling minority not only *should*, according to the democratic ideal, derive its power, both in the constitutional and moral sense, from the mass of the citizens, but that in actual fact it *does* so. It cannot afford in the long run to disregard the primitive sense of justice and self-interest which rules the masses, and sometimes results in changes quite unexpected to, or even contrary to the will of the ruling group.

Disbelief in the Freedom of the Press

In the same trend of thought the author holds the view that in a democracy the so-called free press is but a modern way of influencing and commanding the masses, and the political parties are bound to degenerate into mere objects of power for the politicians:

> The contemporary English-American politics have created through the press a force-field of world-wide intellectual and financial tensions, in which every individual unconsciously takes up the place allotted to him. He must think, will and act as a ruling personality somewhere or other in the distance thinks fit. [Vol. II, Ch. XII, IV, p. 460.]

With reference to a British newspaper magnate, Spengler says:

> . . . the dictator of the press keeps the slavegang of his readers under the whip of his leading articles, telegrams and pictures. What the Press wills is true. Its commanders evoke, transform, interchange truths. Three weeks of press-work and the truth is acknowledged by everybody. [*Ibid.*, p. 461.]

Although there is, again, some truth in Spengler's statement about the undue influence of some press magnates, his statement in its sweeping generality is definitely wrong, as is proven, e.g. by the fact that both in 1940 and in 1948 the result of the U.S. presidential elections was directly contrary to what the overwhelming majority of the American press had predicted or advocated.

Superiority of the Man-of-Action over the Man-of-Thought

Spengler makes a sharp distinction between the man-of-destiny, the "fact man," the political man on the one hand, and the doctrinaire, the thinker, the intellectual on the other hand. He does not hide his deep respect for the former, and his contempt for the latter when discussing this subject. [Vol. II, Chapter I, Section V.]

> There are born destiny-men and causality-men. A whole world separates the purely living man—peasant and warrior, statesman and general, man of the world and man of business, everyone who wills to prosper, to rule, to fight and to dare, the organiser or entrepreneur, the adventurer or bravado or gambler—from the man who is destined either by the power of his mind or the defect of his blood to be an "intellectual"—the saint, priest, savant, idealist, or ideologue . . . there has rarely been a man of any significance in whom the one side or the other has not markedly predominated.
>
> In the last resort, only the active man, the man of destiny, lives in the actual world, the world of political, military and economic decisions, in which concepts and systems do not figure or count. Here a shrewd blow is more than a shrewd conclusion, and there is sense in the contempt with which statesmen and soldiers of all times have regarded the "ink-slinger" and "bookworm" who think that world-history exists for the sake of the intellect or science or even art. [Vol. II, Ch. I, V, pp. 16-17.]

According to Spengler neither Plato nor Rousseau had any influence on the course of history; only the men-of-the-deed such as Alexander, Caesar and Napoleon had.

We may limit ourselves to two remarks in this respect. Could or would Napoleon have succeeded if he had not been able to draw upon the forces unleashed by Voltaire and Rousseau? Would Lenin or Stalin have achieved their results if they had not been able to reap the harvest sown by Karl Marx?

In the second place Spengler overlooks the possibility that the two elements may sometimes be combined in one man. In fact, if the greatness of statesmen is measured not by the number of battles fought, but by the wisdom shown and the lasting blissful effects created, then the greatest appear to be exactly those who combined force of action with force of the spirit: Pericles, William the Silent, Benjamin Franklin, Abraham Lincoln, Disraeli, Thomas Masaryk, Woodrow Wilson, Winston Churchill, Sun Yat-sen, Gandhi. Even the idols of Prussianism, like Frederick the Great, Bismarck and Hitler only played the part on the world stage which they did exactly because they combined action with vision.

Consistent in his trend of thought Spengler ignores and denies the influence of spiritual forces and especially that of religion on the course of history:

"A religion has never yet altered the style of an existence."

What, one may be tempted to ask, about the preachings of Christ? Or of Mohammed? Or of Buddha?

Neither Morality nor Justice, Only Force Counts in Politics

Spengler proclaims the immunity of political behavior from morality, a favorite theme with German thinkers and politicians from Luther to Hitler.

The born statesman stands beyond true and false. He does not confuse the logic of events with the logic of systems. . . . He has convictions, certainly, that are dear to him, but he has them as a private person; no real politician ever felt himself tied to them when in action. [Vol. II, Ch. XII, II, p. 440.]

No doubt Genghis Khan and Hitler considered themselves beyond true and false; but William the Silent and George Washington certainly did not.

Spengler goes even one step further than proclaiming the amorality of all politics: he also contends that those who stand for justice and truth are always bound to be beaten by those who put their faith in power. In his hardly concealed contempt for the former forces, his typical appreciation of values stands out with a belief in "race" and "cosmic force" as the only really creative forces.

World history is the world court. It has ever decided in favour of the stronger, fuller and more self-assured life. Always it has sacrificed truth and justice to might and race, and passed doom of death upon men and peoples to whom truth was more than deeds, and justice than power. [Vol. II, Ch. XIV, III, p. 507.]

Although it is undeniable that power plays a tremendous role in history and in politics, Spengler commits the mistake typical of the Hitlers of all times, of underestimating the power of spiritual forces in the long run; yet it is by these very forces that in the end they are wrecked.

These are some of the prejudices which characterize Spengler's appraisal of values.

Everyone is, of course, entitled to his own outlook on life and his own set of values. When, however, an author allows these to influence his scientific work to a degree where he tries to enforce them as a universal standard for all times and all nations, everyone who accepts the value of Christian ethics or of the democratic form of society must reject them as vigorously as they have been put forward. One is even *obliged* to do so in a case where the author's conclusions, partly as a result of these prejudices, have had such a nefarious effect on the self-confidence of a whole civilization as Spengler's.

At the same time one should try to assess the value of his construction, divorced from these prejudices, of the cyclical course of civilizations.

This construction itself has also been subject to serious objections. Prominent among these are the following.

THE MAIN COUNTS OF CRITICISM

The Fallacy of a Pattern in History

The contention that it is impossible and therefore useless for the human mind to try to detect a purposeful pattern in history has always been the most effective argument, and the one most difficult to disprove, against any attempt to array the facts of history in a specific pattern. The same objection was to be raised again with respect to a subsequent great attempt, this time by a professional historian, who devoted a special discussion to its refutation. For this reason we shall defer a discussion of this objection to Chapters VI and VII.

Exaggerated Use of Parallelism Between Civilizations

The view that history is made up of civilizations which are born, grow, decay and die according to a constantly recurring pattern has equally been subjected to fundamental attack. Here, as in so many respects, Spengler has defeated his own purpose by pushing the parallel between different civilizations to such extremes and applying it to such details that it often does not convince and even invites ridicule. Comparisons are helpful as long as one remembers that they apply to essentials only, the details of two historic occurrences never being 100 per cent alike. This is what Spengler forgot. By trying to carry the parallel so far as to prove the synonymity of specific facts and personalities in different civilizations* he obscured the real question, which is whether there exists a similarity in general trends and stages of development, in other words a similarity *in essentials*, between the phases of different civilizations. The same question will come up again in a less confused form in connection with Toynbee's theories, since the latter did limit the similarity to these essentials. It seems preferable, therefore, to postpone an answer on this point, too, until we consider Toynbee's views on the matter.

Spengler's Mythical View of History

One of Spengler's axioms is that the world-of-history, unlike the world-of-nature, is driven by forces beyond all rules of causality and even beyond the reach of scientific analysis. History is deter-

* For examples see Huizinga, *Verzamelde Werken*, 4, pp. 451 a. ff.; Sorokin, *op. cit.*, pp. 84 a. ff.

mined by *Schicksal*, an almost untranslatable German word which stands for an emotional and mythical concept of fate, which has moved the German soul from the tragic end in the Nibelungen saga to the dramatic suicide and burning of Adolf Hitler in the Reichschancellery; it is Destiny with a capital D, by preference with a heavily dramatic finale of self-destruction. This element must be taken into consideration in assessing the true value of Spengler's conclusions, since it is largely responsible for his prediction of the inevitably approaching doom of our civilization.

The view that all history is determined by fate implies a severely deterministic attitude: each civilization is destined, even before its inception, by fate to follow a rigidly prescribed path; every attempt to deflect from that path is not only senseless, but foolish, and, according to Spengler, cowardice. The strong man accepts his Destiny and undergoes it.

The trouble is that the only revelation we possess of this Destiny is Spengler's work; he admits of no other interpretations. We have to take his word for it that this is the will of fate. Since history is in his opinion not subject to the laws of exact science or of causality, it is no use to try to deduct the future from the past. Yet, inconsistently, this is exactly what Spengler is constantly trying to do, although he does not draw his conclusions from an understandable causality of events but from a certain recurring pattern revealed by history and therefore apparently willed by Destiny.

This belief in a metaphysical Destiny is again a highly subjective outlook and as such a matter of personal faith rather than of science. However, on the one hand to deny, like Spengler, all possibility of reasonable understanding and of causal explanation of history, and on the other hand to demand that mankind submit blindly to a Destiny as interpreted by Spengler, is a road which few have been prepared to follow.

No matter whether one accepts a superhuman plot in the

story of mankind or not, it abounds with the determined efforts of individuals and groups and nations which, as far as man can judge, have changed the course of events.

Exaggerated Use of the Metaphor of Organic Life

The deterministic character of Spengler's view of history, already strong on account of his belief in the force of Destiny, is further intensified by his rigidly organic concept of civilizations: he not only *compares* them to organic beings, but actually ascribes to them qualities which a plant or human being would possess. His metaphor of birth, youth, maturity and death, of spring, summer, autumn and winter of a civilization assumes a significance far beyond that of a mere comparison. It assumes a compelling character. Instead of using it as a convenience to make his ideas more clearly understood, the author gets caught in his own metaphor and becomes its slave instead of its master. His civilizations possess a life of their own; they adopt attitudes with regard to other cultures, are afraid of aging; they use statesmen and nations for the fulfillment of their destiny.

In Spengler's conception of civilizations as living beings man is reduced to a will-less tool in the hands of these civilizations, that is in the hands of Destiny. In this conception it would indeed be folly for man to refuse to accept the dictum of death passed upon Western civilization by Judge Spengler in the name of the eternal justice of Destiny.

*   *   *

Yet, all this being said, there remains the undeniable fact that Spengler's work is fascinating and significant not only for its brilliance but for the great outlines of civilizations which it reveals. Rarely were genius and romantic superstition more closely interwoven in one work. The critical reader, says Huizinga, continually feels as if he were being taken on a majestic mountain tour by a guide in whose eyes there shimmers the glow of insanity.

Had Spengler, instead of extolling the virtues of military discipline, applied more scientific discipline to his own work, his general theme about the uniform life course of all civilizations would have emerged in a much clearer and more convincing form. He overdid himself by trying to bring out sharp black and white contrasts where there were only shades of dark and light, by sharpening his distinctions to violent antitheses, by unnecessarily pursuing his parallels into the smallest details, by presenting his views as the revelation of Destiny, and by identifying his civilizations with organic beings. But all that does not vitiate the convincing character of his thesis if divested of all these weaknesses and reduced to a reasonable thesis: there does exist a general similarity in the development of civilizations. As we will see in the following chapters, this thesis finds strong support in the facts and in the works of others.

The refutation of Spengler's views on the many points mentioned in this chapter, furthermore, does not explain away the impressive fact that this man, who started to put his ideas in writing before the first shot of World War I had been fired, foresaw with uncanny vision the advent of the world wars, of mass democracy and of the great dictators, the growth of the world cities, the onset of sterility, the rise of Russia and of Asia. All these developments, the first signs of which were barely perceptible before World War I, have in the course of the ensuing decades borne out the predictions of Spengler. As far as these developments are concerned they are irrefutable proof of the correctness of his general outline of the development of civilizations.

What they do not prove is the correctness of the value which Spengler, on the basis of a militaristic, anti-democratic and unchristian personal outlook, attached to particular times and phenomena. Nor do they prove that the last phase of a civilization is its poorest one, nor, above all, do they prove that the value and duration of that phase are predetermined beyond man's power to add or detract.

V

Arnold Toynbee's View of Civilizations

BARELY twenty years later on the other side of the British
Channel a historian of equal, if not greater dimensions and
wider vision than Spengler, set himself the task of probing into
the laws governing the life and death of civilizations.

If Spengler was intensely and typically German in his approach
of the problem, Toynbee on his part was equally British. Spengler, consciously or unconsciously, tried to constitute a rigid
pattern into which all civilizations had to fit, developing as they
did, in his idea, according to inescapable laws like an organic
being. Toynbee, on the contrary, proceeded along the tested
British path of empiricism, without—or at least meaning to be
without—preconceived ideas.

In addition to, and closely connected with, this difference
springing from national character there is one in outlook—
Spengler is above all a militarist, Toynbee above all a Christian.
We shall revert to this difference in Chapter VII.

Yet, notwithstanding these deep-rooted differences, Toynbee
too perceives a certain similarity in the development of different
civilizations which induces him to establish in broad outlines
a general—though not unalterable—pattern of that development
not unlike Spengler's. Let us try from the wealth of knowledge
and profusion of facts piled up in the mighty volumes of his
Study of History to trace the main lines of his thoughts.

Toynbee draws into the scope of his study all known civilizations, of which he distinguishes thirty. Of these twenty-one have
achieved full growth; of five, which he calls "arrested civiliza-

tions" the growth has been brought to a standstill before they reached maturity, four others were stillborn ("abortive Civilizations").

Of the twenty-one full-grown civilizations seven are still in existence as living societies. These are: the Hindu, the Islamic, the Far Eastern, the Byzantine or Orthodox Christian in Southeast Europe, the Russian offshoot of that civilization, and the Western civilization. The deceased civilizations which have preceded them are: the Egyptian, the Andean, the Sinic, the Minoan, the Sumeric, the Mayan, the Yucatec, the Mexican (the latter two fused into the Central American), the Hittite, the Syriac, the Babylonic, the Iranic, the Arabic (the latter two fused into the Islamic), and the Hellenic.

THE RHYTHM OF CIVILIZATIONS

As Toynbee slowly and majestically builds up the symphony of his argument there is a fundamental theme which recurs in many variations and which is therefore worth mentioning at the outset before detailing his ideas about the life of civilizations. It is the theme of a constant rhythm, an up and down movement, a swinging of the pendulum which is apparent throughout the development of a civilization, just as well as in that of a country or of an individual, and which makes its influence particularly felt at the critical stages. This rhythm occurs in different forms in Toynbee's theories.

The main form is that of *challenge and response*. In the course of its development a society is repeatedly being faced by challenges to its well-being and even to its very existence. Its response to that challenge determines its future: if the response is adequate to meet the challenge the life of that society will continue enhanced by the internal and external force deriving from its success. If the challenge is not successfully met the society loses in intrinsic value or in external prestige or in material welfare, perhaps even to such an extent as to constitute virtually the end of that particular society.

These repeated challenges and responses constitute ups and downs—or, more correctly, downs and ups—in the life of the society, which occur not only during the phase of growth, but also during that of disintegration. In the latter phase they are characterized by Toynbee as a process of *rout and rally*, or *rally and response*. Essentially this does not seem to be much different from the challenge and response rhythm, the main difference being that during the phases of birth and growth the response is greater than the challenge, bringing the civilization each time to a higher level, whereas during the phases of decay the rally does not quite make up for the rout. In other words: neither the growth nor the disintegration is a process of uninterrupted rise or decline; rather it is a line formed by alternating "secondary" upward and downward movements, which in their entirety make up a rising or declining "primary" movement during the growth or disintegration periods respectively.

A third rhythmic movement which the author sometimes discerns in the life of a society is that of *withdrawal and return*. Again this is a general rhythm in nature, characteristic of creativeness. The seed "withdraws" into the soil and re-emerges in the developed form of a plant. Likewise an individual, a society, a nation or a civilization may at times withdraw from the surrounding world and go through a process of inward purification or development, only to return enriched and strengthened into the company of its similars. Many examples of this phenomenon are given by Toynbee, some of which will be mentioned below.

So much for the rhythm which Toynbee discerns within the life of each civilization, much as it exists in all life on earth. It is, however, a secondary rhythm which takes its place inside a much larger rhythm, a cyclical movement of the appearance, development and disappearance of civilizations, which constitutes the main theme of his masterpiece. He has divided it into four parts, dealing respectively with the birth, the growth, the breakdown and the disintegration of civilizations.

THE BIRTH OF CIVILIZATIONS

The birth of a civilization is ascribed by Toynbee, contrary to many earlier historians, not to the superiority of a particular race, nor to exceptionally favorable surroundings, but rather to exceptionally hard circumstances. Such circumstances constitute a challenge to the society concerned, which the latter will try to meet in order to survive or to maintain its level of well-being. If it successfully meets and overcomes the challenge this stimulus may so much improve its inner strength and creative force as to give birth to what commonly is called "a civilization."

It must be emphasized that although a certain giftedness or inventiveness is needed on the part of the challenged society in order to meet the challenge successfully, Toynbee by no means accepts the racial explanation which ascribes the birth of a civilization to the inherent superiority or genius of a particular race or nation. Rather is it a combination of challenging circumstances on the one hand with the qualities of the society concerned on the other which produces what is as much a miracle in history as the birth of physical life is in the world of nature.

As examples of this process of birth Toynbee points especially to the Egyptian and Sumeric civilizations, the origin of both of which he ascribes to the change of climate which turned the grasslands of the wet and fertile African-Asian plains into dry and barren desert unfit for the inhabitants to continue their hunters' existence. Neither the Nile valley, nor that of the Euphrates and Tigris was by nature a place conducive to prosperity. Proof of this is found in the primitive and poor state in which the inhabitants of the Upper Nile Valley and of the Euphrates-Tigris delta have continued to live up to the present day; yet they live under conditions similar to those which the founders of the Egyptian and Sumeric civilizations must originally have faced when, driven by audacity or desperation, they descended into these jungle swamps.

Another example of Toynbee's thesis is given in the Chinese civilization, which did not originate in the fertile Yangtze valley, but in that of the Yellow River with its swamps and floods.

The origin of the civilizations in question can only be explained by the fact that a particular nation or tribe, forced by circumstances which rendered its traditional dwelling places unfit for living, made a determined effort to convert the swampy valleys in question into fertile ground. Once their effort proved successful the favorable circumstances which they called into being became the womb in which the unleashed productive forces of those nations generated a civilization.

THE GROWTH OF CIVILIZATIONS

Growth of a civilization is, in Toynbee's conception, not a simple and automatic biological process which follows the birth of a civilization. This is proven by the fact that several civilizations have been arrested in the course of just such a process. This may happen, for instance, if the challenge encountered is so severe that in trying to meet it the society consumes all its energy, so that even if the response is successful it leaves insufficient productive forces for further growth.

If, then, the growth of a civilization does not necessarily and automatically follow its birth, what are the characteristics by which such growth can be recognized?

Again Toynbee approaches the answer by first eliminating some obvious possibilities. Neither an expansion of control over territory or people (political or military expansion), nor that over physical environment (improvement of technique) are a phenomenon or proof of growth. Rather is the reverse the case: history shows that the greatest territorial expansion of a civilization usually takes place in the early phase of disintegration, whereas improvement of technique may even kill a civilization, as in the case of the arrested civilizations: the improved technique absorbs all energy, the society becomes its slave instead of its master.

The positive characteristic of a growing civilization, according to Toynbee, is a process of "etherialization." In every field of development—in language, dress, technique, science—he perceives a constantly increasing simplification. As a result ever less energy is required for solving the purely physical problems of life, and ever more energy becomes available for "spiritual" activity. Accordingly a shift takes place in the field where the challenge and response operates: the challenges now derive less from the physical surroundings and more from social or spiritual conflicts within the society. Hence the process of growth becomes one of "self-articulation" or "self-determination."

In this process the movement of withdrawal and return plays an important part. Numerous examples are cited by Toynbee of what he considers temporary withdrawals, either of societies or of their "creative minorities." Thus Athens did not take part in the general Greek colonization which went on between the eighth and sixth centuries B.C., but after that it returned to take the lead in the community of Greek states. Italy withdrew from the feudal community between the thirteenth and fifteenth centuries and during that period achieved the transformation from an agrarian to an urban commercial and industrial society. England during its relative isolation from Europe from the fifteenth to the eighteenth century laid the foundations of parliamentary democracy and modern industrial society. The possibility should not be discounted, according to Toynbee, that the present seclusion of Russia from the outside world constitutes a similar process of temporary withdrawal.

At this stage of Toynbee's narrative appears a conception which in the general trend of his thought is no more than a side line, yet constitutes one of those fascinating crystallizations of which his work is so full. It is his treatise upon the relationship between societies and their leaders, be they individuals or groups. Although rejecting both the view that a society is a living organism of which the individual is just a member, and the view that a society is no more than a collection of single individuals, Toynbee points out that undeniably the source of action in each society rests with individuals or with small minorities; they constitute the *creative minority*. Their problem in relation to the passive, uncreative majority is to make their views prevail and get them put into effect. Since the mass is incapable of mentally and spiritually living through the same experience as the creative minority, the best that can be achieved is an acceptance, and consequently an imitation, by the mass of the outlook and attitude of the leaders. This is the process which Toynbee calls *mimesis*.

Here is a far more subtle and convincing, and in the end far more realistic, explanation of the relationship between leaders and masses than Spengler's crude militaristic division of all societies into rulers and ruled, master and slave, subject and object of power. At first sight one might be inclined to consider the difference one of degree and explanation rather than of substance, the fact being admitted by both Spengler and Toynbee that there *is* in each society a minority which in fact rules and a majority which obeys. However, the allegiance of the majority rests on a fundamentally different basis in the two conceptions, and the consequences of this difference come to light clearly in regard to the breakdown and disintegration of civilizations. According to Toynbee it is an essential phenomenon of disintegration that the leading minority, by falling short in creative leadership, loses its charm over and the allegiance of the masses, and thereupon tries to continue its leadership by enforcing blind obedience. According to Spengler, on the contrary, blind obedience to the leaders is essential to a healthy civilization and its loss consequently fatal. Thus what is essential to the one—blind obedience based on force—is a criterion and cause of decay to the other.

This leads us to the next stage in the life of a civilization: the breakdown which inaugurates the disintegration.

THE BREAKDOWN OF CIVILIZATIONS

Again, Toynbee starts off by repudiating several explanations proffered by earlier historians for these phenomena.

Thus it is not force from outside which causes the collapse of a society. The fact that a society is sometimes defeated by external political or military forces is merely a proof of its internal decay: if similar dangers turn up during the phase of growth they are not only victoriously repelled but often even constitute a stimulus which proves a stepping stone for ascendance to a higher level.

Neither does Toynbee accept the deterministic explanations of history, or the theory that a civilization after a given period necessarily must collapse from racial or spiritual decay.

Furthermore, it follows from his previously mentioned views that, just as improvement of technique or expanded control over the environment does not indicate growth of a civilization, decline of technique or geographic contraction of control over the human environment does not in itself constitute or prove a breakdown.

What does constitute a breakdown is: the failure successfully to answer a particular challenge. Many may be the causes from which such failure springs: the hitherto voluntary "mimesis" of the masses may have turned into either an automatic imitation or an enforced drill; old institutions may fail to be adapted to new purposes; self-complacency or idolization of persons or institutions or techniques may cause a loss of creativity.

In all these different cases the core of the breakdown is the same: *the creative minority can no longer bring up sufficient creative force to meet the challenge of the moment.* As a result it loses its appeal to and its spell over the masses and can only continue to exercise its leadership either by force or by rendering the mimesis automatic and therefore empty. The creative or leading minority thus becomes a dominant or oppressive minority, with the result that the masses, or at least part of them, withdraw their allegiance and end their mimesis; they feel placed outside the society and its civilization, take up an attitude of detachment or hostility to it, and thus become what Toynbee calls an "internal proletariat." Thus a schism in the body politic, a loss of social unity occurs, which is the beginning of disintegration.

Civilization has thus reached its final stage, that of disintegration.

THE DISINTEGRATION OF CIVILIZATIONS

The question whether a breakdown must inevitably lead to disintegration is answered in the negative. There is an alternative: If the schism is healed, if there is a sufficiently strong rally, the process of decay may be arrested and the civilization enter into a stage of petrification, which may last for centuries. This is what happened to the Egyptian and Far Eastern civilizations.

If, however, the disintegration is not nipped in the bud, it will run its course, which is characterized by several phenomena common to the last phase of all civilizations.

TOYNBEE'S CHARACTERISTICS OF THE LAST PHASE OF CIVILIZATION

Schism in the Body Social. Internal and External Proletariat

There appears, first of all, the just mentioned schism in the body social between the "dominant minority" and the "internal proletariat." This challenge from within to the leadership of the disintegrating society is supplemented by one from without, coming from an "external proletariat." Each civilization is constantly being challenged and threatened by civilizations or groups from outside. As long as the civilization is growing and vigorous it will not only meet and overcome those challenges successfully, but will even by its "radiation" exercise a certain spell and influence over those surrounding groups, as a result of which they will consciously or unconsciously follow its leadership. Once, however, the breakdown has occurred, that phenomenon of "radiation and attraction" comes to an end with regard to the external as much as with regard to the internal masses and gives way to the process of challenge and response: the outside groups confront the society with new challenges, and as the dominant minority fails to meet these it loses its spell over the former. As a result these become an external "proletariat," in the Toynbeean sense, meaning a large group which feels placed "outside" society by being underprivileged in an economic or political or social sense, and hence becomes antagonistic to it.

The social and political structure of a civilization in disintegration is therefore marked by a split of the body social into three factions: a dominant minority, opposed by both an internal and an external proletariat. The schism may be horizontal only, i.e., constitute a social or ideological split across frontiers, or it may be vertical, i.e., take the form of a struggle between geographically divided areas or alliances. The two forms may mix, as they do in our time.

Schism in the Soul

Coincident with the schism in the body social, and equally characteristic of the disintegration of a society is a "schism in the soul," which makes itself felt both in the society as a whole and in the individual: creativity is replaced by either abandon or self-control, mimesis by truancy or martyrdom; a sense of drift and a sense of sin replace the former creative *élan*, a sense of promiscuity and a sense of unity the former sense of style; the differentiation which was a mark of growth is replaced by standardization, a mark of decay.

As a remedy the disintegrating society seeks refuge in different forms of escapism, such as: archaism, an attempt to return to the past; futurism, an attempt to leap to a future utopia; detachment, an attempt to withdraw from the world, as exemplified in the teachings of Buddha; transfiguration, an attempt to find the utopia beyond this world, as embodied in the teachings of Christ.

Each of these spiritual attitudes toward the disintegration of society may find its incarnation in prophets who pose as saviors. Thus Toynbee distinguishes the following types of saviors: the creative genius; the "saviour with the sword," i.e., the founders and maintainers of the universal state; the "saviour with the time machine," i.e., he who promises improvement by a return to the past or a jump into the future; the "philosopher masked by a King," Plato's remedy; and finally the God incarnate in a man, the only saviour who conquers death.

Time of Troubles

The disintegration and the schism inherent in it engender a period of great political and social conflicts, known in the Toynbeean terminology as a "time of troubles": heavy and large scale warfare takes place between powerful states, alliances or ideologies. It is total warfare in the modern sense, involving and strongly influencing the life of the whole nation, carried on until the bitter end, aimed not only at the defeat, but at the very annihilation of the opponent and his leaders.

The time of troubles exhausts the warring nations and factions and creates among the masses a growing longing for peace and stability above all. It thus paves the way for the next phenomenon in the process of disintegration: the establishment of a universal state by the strongest state or faction, which finally manages to establish its hegemony over the whole area then covered by the civilization.

Universal State and Universal Church

Insofar as the universal state implies the imposition by a dominant minority of its rule over an unwilling internal proletariat, it carries the seeds of its own destruction within. The universal state is the response of the dominant minority to the challenge to its rule by the internal and external proletariat. The proletariat, however, finds no satisfaction in the universal state since the dominant minority can no longer render its rule sufficiently attractive and convincing; hence the proletariat looks for and develops new ideologies or religions of its own. One of these develops into a "universal church" which thus becomes the proletariat's creative response to the challenge with which the dominant minority has confronted it in the universal state.

The universal state may last for a long time and may during that period conserve the civilization in a state of petrifaction. The universal church lasts still longer and even outlives the civilization itself. But neither of them is capable of reversing the process of disintegration; on the contrary, the universal church, being contrary to the beliefs and very roots of the dominant minority, will tend to undermine the civilization, even though that church may be tolerated or adhered to by the dominant minority itself, as happened with the Christian religion in the last phase of the Roman Empire.

Barbarian Warbands

The external proletariat, on its part, responds to the creation of the universal state by setting up barbarian warbands under the leadership of heroes who find their own ideology in hero worship and epic poetry. These barbarian bands of warriors constantly harassing the frontiers of the universal state are another phenomenon of the last stage of civilization.

Finally the universal state, and with it the civilization which it embodies, as a result of its own weakness succumbs to the combination of the undermining by the universal church and the onslaught of the barbarian bands. The dominant minority has finally lost the battle against the internal and external proletariats; its response to their challenges has been inadequate. Civilization has come to an end.

Interregnum, Voelkerwanderung and Heroic Age

With this event society relapses into its primitive stage until the dawn of a new civilization. This period is therefore considered by Toynbee as an "interregnum" between two civilizations. It is characterized by mass movements of barbarian tribes and peoples of the former universal empire, uprooted from their dwelling places: it is the period of the "Voelkerwanderung," also called "heroic age" because it is dominated by the warlords and heroes whom we find in the primitive stage of each society.

Much of the former civilization disappears in this interregnum. But not all of it. It is here that the universal church, created by the internal proletariat, starts to play a historic part of inestimable value. For the universal church, not really being "of" the old civilization, does not die with it; it "withdraws" during the interregnum, only to re-emerge as the generating force of a new civilization; it is the cocoon in which the essence of civilization is preserved, in order that another civilization, of greater beauty and higher development, may be born from it. Thus the eternal cycle of life and death is completed; a civilization has died, but in its death has brought forth the germ from which new and richer life may spring. And as this miracle has again unrolled itself before the mortal eye, it leaves us helpless before the eternal enigma which man has tried to solve ever since the spark of reason started to glow in his mind: Why? What is the sense of this—if there is any sense or purpose in it at all? And if there is such a purpose, is it possible for the human eye to detect it?

This leads straight to the deepest root of the criticism that can and has been leveled against Toynbee's work, and which deserves our attention before drawing conclusions.

VI

Discussion of Toynbee's Views

IT SHOULD not surprise that at a time when Western civilization has come to doubt itself and its future, the teachings of Toynbee have aroused an interest and collected a following seldom equaled in the field of history.

The stir caused by Spengler's *Decline of the West* in the nineteen-twenties was a typical postwar phenomenon of World War I. The still greater impact of World War II has given rise to a still greater sense of crisis in the Western world; the geographic expansion and shift of the field of military action has entailed a corresponding expansion and shift of the field of interest: Spengler found his sounding board primarily on the European continent, Toynbee in the Anglo-Saxon world.

Elaborate has been the discussion and manifold the criticism to which Toynbee's ideas have given rise. Yet even most of his critics have bowed in tribute to his encompassing knowledge in the field of history, the deepness of his insight, and the mastery of his design. None has been able, or even attempted, to overthrow or rival his construction by one of equal scope.

In order to judge the real strength of this mighty tower of theory it seems necessary to scan the field of criticism surrounding it.

THE MAIN COUNTS OF CRITICISM

There Is No Pattern or Purpose in History

The most fundamental criticism of the pattern laid down in *A Study of History* is the contention that the course of history, in its immense richness and eternal variety, can never be reduced to a more or less standard pattern. This objection has been raised by nearly all those who criticize Toynbee's work, be it in varying degrees. It is a conviction common to most historians of the last century and to many of the present that history is ever changing, and therefore ever unpredictable. Furthest in this respect go those who contend that it is beyond human capacity to establish whether there is any sense in history at all, and if so, to grasp it. Others, while admitting that it is possible and imperative for the historian to try to discern a sense in history, assert that that sense can never constitute a rigid and inflexible pattern which inexorably repeats itself.

Toynbee's reply is that he, too, does not believe in a rigid and inflexible pattern, and that he has never tried to establish one. On the contrary, he insists that his approach is purely empirical, and that if that approach has led him to discover a certain uniformity in the development of civilizations, that uniformity should never be considered as constituting an unalterable path which all civilizations are predestined to follow. On the other hand he insists with equal force that he does not share what he calls "the non-sense view of history fashionable among Western historians for the last few generations," and that there is no reason why one should not try to make sense of the facts of history. In his radio discussion with Professor Geyl, who contended that this was an impossible task, he said: "We can't afford such defeatism; it is unworthy of the greatness of man's mind; and it is refuted by the human mind's past achievements. . . . This job of making sense of history is one of the crying needs of our day."

This difference of outlook as to whether history can and should be interpreted so as to make sense or not is fundamental; it basically determines one's attitude toward Toynbee's theories: those who hold that history defies meaningful interpretation by the human mind find it obviously difficult to accept Toynbee's sketch of the broad lines along which civilizations develop, and still more difficult to accept Spengler's biological determinism or Marx's historical materialism.

In turn one's attitude as to the sense or non-sense of history is, obviously, to a great extent determined by one's religious and spiritual conceptions and therefore defies scientific discussion.

Toynbee's Christian "Bias"

This brings us to the second reason for which some historians have taken exception to Toynbee's teachings: that they are not the result of purely scientific research, but in the final analysis are dictated by his religious convictions. This reproach is expressed most tersely by the American sociologist H. E. Barnes:

> *A Study of History* is really a grandiose and majestic revival of what George Santayana has called "the Christian Epic" as expounded by Augustine and his associates. . . .
> To unfold the drama of the past damnation and possible ultimate salvation of humanity, not sober and direct historical exposition, is the primary aim of Toynbee. [H. E. Barnes, "Arnold Toynbee: Orosius and Augustine in Modern Dress," in *An Introduction to the History of Sociology*, p. 719.]
> The process and stages through which societies have perished without the True Faith constitute both the theory and action of *A Study of History* [*Ibid*. p. 721.]

To anyone who has read Toynbee it must be obvious that this is not a fair rendering of his thinking. While he makes it plain that he is guided by his Christian convictions, and that indeed in his opinion the survival of Western civilization depends upon a revival of the Christian faith, it is equally obvious that by no means does Toynbee ascribe the fall of other civilizations to a failure to observe the "True Faith," nor do his conclusions about the usual phases of a civilization in any way derive from his religious views.

Yet when the allegation of Christian "bias" is reduced to its true character, which is more that of a "basis" than a "bias," it is fundamentally correct and must be answered. To this two replies can in our opinion be made.

The first is that there seems to be no reason why a scientist who is guided by the Christian faith is for that reason more biased or less scientific than one who is guided by Wellsian faith in the power of Reason, by Spenglerian faith in Destiny, by Romein's faith in Marxist doctrine or by someone else's faith in democracy. Rather is the conclusion from the foregoing that in fields of science so close to the fundamental issues of life no purely "scientific" answer is possible. In other words willingly or unwillingly almost every scientist is guided by certain principles or outlook or "bias," whatever one may choose to call them. We shall leave aside here the deeper question whether pure "science for science's sake" has brought forth such valuable fruit for mankind as to make any moral strings attached to it rejectable.

In the second place it would seem that even for someone seeking to establish historic truth on the basis of pure facts it is very well possible to accept certain conclusions from the facts arrayed by Toynbee without accepting his Christian principles, in the same way as it was possible to accept many of Spengler's conclusions without sharing his militarist outlook. The value and truth of the great majority of Toynbee's findings, particularly regarding the similarity in the development of different civilizations, is not, it seems to us, dependent upon the acceptance or rejection of his Christian conviction.

Civilizations Are Not Born and Do Not Wholly Die

A third fundamental challenge to Toynbee's theory—and to those of Danilevsky and Spengler as well—is that the whole metaphor of civilizations being born, growing, maturing and disintegrating, though attractive at first sight because of its simplicity, is inapplicable simply because civilizations are not born and do not die. According to these critics a civilization is not an integrated system, not a consistent and closely knit unity, but a conglomeration of cultural phenomena—political, economic, scientific, religious, social, etc.—which can be transferred from one civilization to another. Although a number of these phenomena combine at certain periods to constitute what we call a civilization, some of them may have existed before the civilization appeared or may survive after its disappearance. This implies that a civilization is not really born and never dies entirely.

According to this trend of thought, as expressed by Sorokin, Graeco-Roman civilization, for instance, is still alive in the classic Greek authors and philosophies, in Roman law and in Roman forms and methods of government.

A multitude of cultural values of Graeco-Roman "civilization" are still imitated, practiced and incorporated in our civilization, culture and institutions, in our mentality, conduct and relationships. They live, function and influence us, being much more alive than last year's best seller or yesterday's fads and fashions. . . . None of the "great civilizations" is dead in toto. . . . With a reasonable degree of certainty one may claim that a substantial percentage of any of the foregoing "dead" civilizations —in some cases a very large percentage—is still very much alive.

Critical scrutiny of this thesis shows it to be a fallacy. The fact that Homer and Plato are still being read and Roman law is still being studied and applied does not mean that classic civilization itself is still *alive*. Neither does the fact that we wear pajamas and drink coffee prove that Ottoman civilization is still alive. An author can be dead even though his books are still widely read, or a painter if his paintings are still admired. A tea plant may be dead though its leaves are still being used to make tea. The test of life or death is whether it is still possible to produce new forms or products. In this there is indeed no difference between a living organism and a culture, however much the comparison may have been abused in other respects. Since the disintegration of Greece and Rome no new Greek literature has been written, no new Greek architectural forms have been developed, no new Roman law has been created. Later authors have written in Greek or Latin and may conceivably still do so today, later architects have constructed neo-classic buildings and later glossators have interpreted and commented on Roman law; but none of these products were "part" of Greek or Roman civilization. That civilization is dead, because it no longer develops, grows, creates; it does not produce new manifestations or creations; it no longer *lives*. That is not changed by the circumstance that many of its past creations are still valuable parts of our cultural heritage.

The first of the three fundamental objections discussed up to now, namely that Toynbee forcibly attempts to make sense of history, also constitutes the source of most other objections that have been leveled against his work.

Prophet of Gloom?

Another reproach, for instance, made by Professor Geyl in his radio debate with Toynbee, is that the latter's conception tends to induce unnecessary gloom about the future of Western civilization.

To this Toynbee has quite justly retorted that the "gloomy" or "cheerful" quality of a theory has nothing to do with its being true or false. If an unbiased appraisal of the facts leads to a gloomy conclusion it is sheer cowardice to reject that conclusion on the mere ground of its being gloomy.

There is, however, a more fundamental answer to the argument. Toynbee's view of history would really induce gloom only if it implied that our civilization is doomed and in the process of going down an inescapable road of disintegration and decay, in other words if it implied predestination. This Toynbee emphatically denies. He is, in his own words, "at the opposite pole, on that supremely important question, from the famous German philosopher Spengler." (*Can We Know the Pattern of the Past?*, p. 20.)

In Toynbee's view the course of history is the resultant of a process of challenge and response, and if there is plenty in our recent history to warrant a sense of uneasiness, this should only constitute "a challenging call to action, not a death sentence to paralyze our wills." (*Ibid.* p. 22.)

One-sided Choice or Presentation of Examples

Further attacks upon Toynbee's work are directed against his one-sidedness. This attack takes several closely related forms.

One is that although Toynbee liberally illustrates his theories by numerous examples taken from the history of all times and regions, these examples are chosen arbitrarily from an infinite number of events in order to support Toynbee's theories. It might well be that someone else with as extensive a knowledge could cite as many other cases against these theories; in other words, although Toynbee believes himself to be unprejudiced, he in reality selects his illustrations to suit his case.

Other critics contend that even the facts chosen could often be presented in a slightly or totally different way with the result that they would no longer support the argument, or even plead against it. A notable example of this is furnished by the comeback which Egyptian civilization made after the restoration of the universal state in the New Empire in the sixteenth century B.C., long after it had, according to Toynbee, experienced its "breakdown" and even after the country had already been occupied by foreign barbarians, the Hyksos. Toynbee explains this comeback as a "petrifaction" of a civilization, an epilogue which may preserve it for long time after its disintegration has set in. Yet many historians cannot dismiss the impression that in reality the late course of Egyptian civilization does not quite fit in Toynbee's scheme, and that he uses a somewhat forced explanation to make it tally. Other examples to be mentioned in the next chapter point to a similar conclusion, and many more have been enumerated by Prof. Geyl in his article on "Toynbee's System of Civilizations" (*Journal of the History of Ideas*, January, 1948, reprinted in *The Pattern of the Past*).

In the same vein most of his critics point out that Toynbee bases his general conclusions on the development of Hellenic civilization and tries to make all other societies fit in the Hellenic model.

> He uses Hellenic civilization as the type or pattern for the formulation of his general theory of the rise, growth and decline of all civilizations, frequently having to squeeze his facts into a pattern and framework which they do not always fit. . . .
>
> The main defect of Toynbee's work, aside from its fundamentally theological purpose and orientation, lies in the fact that he had reached his main conclusions before he had got past his synthesis of Hellenic historical experience and had really begun his survey of the twenty-one civilizations that he formally examines. [H. E. Barnes, *op. cit.*, p. 721.]

Again another form of the same reproach is that Toynbee achieves the lucidity and simplicity of his picture by oversimplification of the factors at play. He thus obtains a clearer, easier to understand, and more attractive picture, but is it quite in accordance with reality? Nearly all historians who have discussed Toynbee's work have pointed out with many examples that often it is not. Professor Locher expresses the views of many of his colleagues when he says:

> Heavier than all other objections to Toynbee's concrete interpretations weighs the following: that he simplifies history almost down to mythology. No matter how many fine remarks he makes, how many shades he applies, ever again we find complicated processes reduced to an interplay of a few forces, in which the acting groups assume the shape of simple thinking and reacting creatures. [Th. J. G. Locher, "Toynbee's Antwoord," *De Gids*, May, 1948, p. 119.]

Both on the authority of these historians and on the basis of the facts of history it seems undeniable that Toynbee, notwithstanding the wide margin of variations which he allows, does oversimplify. In the next chapters we will mention some examples showing more variety in the phases of maturity and disintegration than Toynbee's scheme would allow. Yet, even this does not invalidate the whole theory in its general outline. All these attacks are directed primarily against the examples chosen by Toynbee or against the way he uses them, rather than against his general line of thought. Even if, on the basis of as wide a knowledge of the facts of history as Toynbee's, one should have to conclude that certain of his examples have been arbitrarily chosen or presented in a one-sided way so as to fit the theory, it still does not follow that the whole of that theory is necessarily wrong, as long as on the basis of established facts it makes sense in its *general* outlines, as indeed it does. Every great new theory has upon closer scrutiny been shown to contain certain mistakes or exaggerations on secondary, or even on primary points. This does not annul its value, nor does it prove the theory to be wrong in essence.

Neglect of Certain Factors in History

Related to the reproach of one-sidedness is criticism on a sixth score: Certain historians blame Toynbee for paying far too little attention to art, an important aspect of civilization. Others blame him for almost entirely neglecting such important aspects as science, technical development and economics in general and for not taking into account the history of science, economic history, cultural anthropology, historical sociology, and social history. This is a result of his conviction that only spiritual and political forces determine the great trends of history, but he does not give sufficient consideration to what are vital elements in the life of civilizations and indispensable factors for any forecast of what may happen to our civilization.

If correct this objection would be of a very fundamental nature; in particular the neglect of technology and economy in history is insurmountable to those who adhere to the school of historic materialism.

However, the reproach does not seem justified if one realizes, only to mention the main examples, that Toynbee traces the origin of Egyptian civilization to the challenge of hard economic surroundings, its breakdown to the excessive detraction of manpower and energy for the building of the pyramids, the ascendance of Athens to the solution it found for its overpopulation, and the breakdown of Roman society to the latifundia or great estates. In fact in his sequence of challenge and response the challenges are in the early stages very often of an economic nature (the stimulus of hard terrain or of new ground).

What these critics really object to is that Toynbee does not share their belief in the overriding or exclusively decisive importance of economic, technical or material factors, or in the supremacy of reason. These beliefs constitute as much of a "bias" as they reproach Toynbee with.

A Civilization Not the Intelligible Unit of Historical Study

The alleged neglect of the history of science and of economic history is the basis of yet another objection.

One of the bases of Toynbee's *study* is that "the intelligible unit of historical study is neither a nation state nor (at the other end of the scale) mankind as a whole, but a certain grouping of humanity which we have called a society." (Somervell, *Abridgment of Volumes I-VI of A Study of History by Arnold J. Toynbee,* p. 17.)

This basic conception has been assailed on the ground that just as little as the history, say of England, can be understood without that of Western civilization in general, as little can that of Western civilization be understood without taking into consideration the Hellenic or Arabic civilizations.

This basic assumption has also been thought to result from Toynbee's underrating of the influence of science and economics on history. If these factors were taken into account more properly they would reveal, according to the critics, long-term trends and developments not limited to one civilization, but stretching over several civilizations successively or simultaneously.

It seems only fair to Toynbee to point out that although he does indeed take the civilization as the intelligible unit of historical study, his work proves sufficiently how well he is aware of the interrelationship of civilizations. We are even promised two separate volumes on *Contact between Civilizations*. This in itself should be sufficient to prove that, although he calls a society the intelligible unit of historical study, he by no means overlooks the influence of societies upon each other.

Confusing Notion of the Breakdown of Civilizations

Finally we come to a theorem of the great historian which lends itself to what seems to us the most justified criticism. Although this is not of such a basic character as to overthrow the whole of his gigantic structure, it is of considerable importance with regard to any application to our present civilization and therefore deserves particular attention. This is his conception of the *breakdown* of civilizations.

The way he handles this conception is open to criticism in two respects, one regarding the timing, the other regarding the character and effect of a breakdown.

With respect to the timing it has been justly pointed out that in many cases Toynbee places his breakdowns surprisingly early in the life of a civilization. Three instances will suffice to demonstrate this.

The breakdown of the Hellenic civilization according to Toynbee occurred in 431 B.C. with the beginning of the Peloponnesian wars. No doubt it can be argued on good grounds that that event constituted the beginning of the end for *Greece*, but if one considers Greek and Roman civilization as one, as Toynbee does, then it would mean that the whole creative achievement of constructing what finally became the Roman Empire, with all it implied in the way of statecraft, legislation, art, philosophy, simply would form part of the process of decline of Hellenic society.

The same applies to the Orthodox-Russian civilization. This finds its origin in the tenth century. Its breakdown is marked, according to Toynbee, by the decay of the Kiev Kingdom in the thirteenth century, and its time of troubles starts in 1075. Thus this civilization would have had a growth period of hardly a century.

Still more striking is an application to our Western civilization. Toynbee has not yet expressed his final and conclusive answer to the question whether Western civilization has yet broken down. We must await the study which he has promised on this subject. Yet, at several points he has given the impression—and is so understood by some of his colleagues—of considering our society as one that "has broken down and gone into disintegration." (See *A Study of History*, V, p. 193; see also IV, p. 52, 122 and V, p. 403.) This breakdown would then have occurred as long ago as the sixteenth century, with the wars of religion. As Geyl has put it: "The last four centuries of our history would thus, according to your system, be one long process of disintegration." (*Can We Know the Pattern of the Past?*, p. 16.)

From these examples, which are only a few of those given by the critics, one can draw the following conclusion with regard to Toynbee's handling of the *breakdown*: *either* he places his breakdowns too early in time, *or* he uses the word "breakdown" in a sense apt to cause confusion.

This leads us to the other aspect of his "breakdown" theory: what is the meaning, the effect of a breakdown in the Toynbeean terminology? The word in itself, and, in fact, the way he uses it, would tend to suggest that a breakdown constitutes the turning point in the life of a civilization, the event which marks the cleavage between the period of growth and that of decline. Thus employed, the term would constitute the "point of no return" of a civilization, a major crisis or mistake, from which it is never able entirely to recover.

If such is the connotation of the word "breakdown," it follows that once the breakdown has occurred a civilization is doomed to go down the path of disintegration; although there may be "rallies," these are never strong enough to overcome the effects of the initial great "rout." The breakdown thus assumes the character of a metaphysical event, and Toynbee's theory almost reverts to the idea of predestination, which he himself so emphatically rejects; for if "breakdown" is used in the sense of an event from which a society never recovers, then this comes very close to saying that that society is from the moment of the breakdown on doomed, or predestined to die. Toynbee shrinks from this deduction, yet it is the logical consequence of his "breakdown" idea as applied to former civilizations.

We must respect, however, the historian's own statement that he does not admit of any predestination in history. This necessarily implies that a recovery is possible at any moment, even after the breakdown. With regard to our present civilization he says:

> There is nothing to prevent our Western civilization from following historical precedent, if it chooses, by committing social suicide. But we are not doomed to make history repeat itself; it is open to us through our own efforts, to give history, in our case, some new and unprecedented turn. As human beings, we are endowed with this freedom of choice, and we cannot shuffle off our responsibility upon the shoulders of God or nature. We must shoulder it ourselves. It is up to us. . . .
>
> We are not just at the mercy of inexorable fate. [Civilization on Trial, pp. 39 and 41.]

"Breakdown" in this sense assumes an entirely different connotation: it is not a catastrophe beyond redemption, but merely the origin of the shortcomings which finally cause the collapse of

the society. It is then no more than the earliest major event in
the chain of causality to which the ultimate fall can *afterward*
be traced back, much like the earliest symptom of an illness in
the human body, if the body finally collapses as a result of that
illness. That, however, is entirely different from a catastrophe
beyond repair. If a man dies of pneumonia, it may well have been
that he could have survived if, say, his heart had been stronger,
or if he had paid more attention to that initial cold. Yet few will
call that initial cold the breakdown of his physical health.

Nor does a "breakdown" thus conceived even mean that a
society may not stage a comeback and go on to grow and improve after it has occurred. A man may die at forty from a tuber-
culosis of which the first symptoms were noticeable in his child-
hood; yet that did not prevent him from growing to manhood,
and perhaps he might even have lived to be seventy if the illness
had been detected and cured in time. The word "breakdown"
interpreted in this sense assumes an entirely different and less
fatal significance than in the usual sense of the word which
Toynbee, too, often seems to imply.

This duality in his use of the word is well summarized by
Professor Locher when speaking about the breakdown of Hellenic
civilization:

> One out of two: *either* 431 was a *faux pas* which could be remedied,
> but then it did not constitute a breakdown in the Toynbeean sense; *or*
> it did, but then we get a construction by which the entire further history
> of Greek-Roman civilization is beyond salvation as a result of that one
> mistake. This means something like the fall of man. I refuse to accept this;
> this is historical metaphysics. [*Toynbee's Antwoord*, p. 123.]

The unsolved duality in Toynbee's concept of a "breakdown"
is by no means limited to that phenomenon: it is prevalent
throughout his work; it has its roots in a duality of his fundamental attitude, which on the one hand implies that civilizations
normally do conform to a certain broad pattern, and on the other
hand emphasizes that at any moment they can move either up

or down. It is the struggle in his soul between determinism and empiricism, to which we have pointed before, and which adds to his greatness, springing as it does from the struggle for truth.

Yet the existence of this confusing duality must be clearly realized and its effects envisaged, for the latter are of vital importance to any conclusions to be drawn with regard to Western civilization: If a "breakdown" is an irreparable catastrophe, the irrevocable beginning of the end, then it is of vital importance to know whether the breakdown of Western civilization has yet occurred. If so, it means that our civilization is indeed doomed as Spengler proclaimed. If, on the other hand, a breakdown means not more than the first symptom of the disease to which the death of a civilization can in retrospect be traced back, then it loses its ominous significance. For then it would have been possible to cure the disease, if only the right diagnosis had been made in time, the right remedy applied, and the patient possessed sufficient stamina. If "breakdown" is used with that connotation, then it is possible for a society to produce some of its richest fruit after the so-called "breakdown" has occurred. Since the facts show this to be the case in several of the instances mentioned by Toynbee—the New Empire of Egypt after the building of the great pyramids, the Roman Republic and Empire after the Peloponnesian wars, Western Europe after the breakdown which may have occurred in the sixteenth, or even in the eleventh century—we believe that the second interpretation of the word has to be accepted if Toynbee's construction is to make any sense. In fact Professor Toynbee has assured this author that that is how he intended the word to be understood.

Important though the question of the breakdown is, especially with regard to still living civilizations, again it does not destroy the theory as a whole, nor even any of its vital components. Even if the real breakdown, that is the fall from which no redemption is possible, should in a number of societies have occurred much later than the event indicated as such by Toynbee, even then his general scheme of things still stands.

We have now recounted eight major grounds on which Toynbee's theories have been attacked by his fellow historians.

It seems justified to conclude, on the basis of the grounds summarized in the preceding pages, that all but the first are either insufficiently substantiated or not of such a fundamental nature as to defeat the main body of Toynbee's theories.

It is different with the first: If really history is too complicated and too varied for us to detect any general pattern or sense in it, then indeed the whole of Toynbee's carefully built and crystal clear construction crumples to nothing but brilliant, yet incoherent splinters.

The decisive question, therefore, remains whether a general pattern can be detected in the life of civilizations. We will consider that question in the next chapter.

VII

Synthesis: The Pattern of Civilizations

IN THE first part of this book, which is now drawing to a close, we have tried to establish a scientifically reliable basis for an investigation into the present stage and future possibilities of our civilization. We have given a succinct picture of one of the earliest and of the two latest and greatest attempts that have been made to draw up a consistent philosophy about the life and death of civilizations. All the three authors discussed have arrived at what is called a cyclical or rhythmic view of history.

In addition many other important attempts, not based on a cyclical view of history, have been made to explain the rise and fall of civilization. The Russian-born philosophers Berdyaev and Sorokin, the Americans Northrop and Kroeber, to mention only these few, have dug deeply into the same field. It is interesting that, without accepting the cyclical concept of history, some of their views, particularly with regard to the phases through which a civilization passes, have tended to support a good deal of the general outlines of the cyclist theories. Sorokin, after a careful analysis of the philosophies of both schools, arrives at the conclusion that "the real disagreement between the two groups of writers is considerably less than appears at the surface. Their agreement is significant." (Sorokin, *op. cit.*, p. 294.)

We have limited ourselves to a discussion of Danilevsky's, Spengler's and Toynbee's views because they present the most complete and clear-cut explanations of the life of civilizations and have consequently had the strongest general appeal. We shall only occasionally refer to the views of other writers, where the course of the argument so requires.

In trying to come to conclusions it seems most fruitful primarily to compare the two towering projects that dwarf all other attempts made hitherto. Even Danilevsky, interesting though he is as an early precursor, is less important because he did not go nearly so deeply into the matter as Spengler and Toynbee.

There are many and deep-rooted differences between them. Probably the most fundamental of these is the difference in outlook on life. Spengler is above all a militarist, Toynbee above all a Christian. To Spengler the ultimate deciding factor in history is force, and the only sense of history is in the survival of the strongest; to Toynbee there is a moral purpose in history, which is to carry human life from the level of "subman" through that of "man" to that of "higher-than-man." To Spengler, the mili-

tarist, war and militarism are the creator, to Toynbee, the
Christian, they are the destroyer of great things. To Spengler
neither politics nor history is subject to any moral laws, to Toynbee they are both subject to the laws of God.

This difference in philosophy puts its hallmark on both masterpieces. It leads to important differences in results. For instance:
to Spengler the end of Roman civilization sets in after the battle
of Actium in 31 B.C., because from then on large-scale fighting
ended in the Roman realm. To Toynbee, on the contrary, the
end of Hellenic (including Roman) civilization sets in with the
Peloponnesian wars in 431 B.C., because from then on large-scale
fighting between the Greek city-states *started* and prevented them
from uniting, thus spelling their downfall.

If Spengler was intensely and typically German in his approach
to the problem, Toynbee on his part is equally British. Spengler,
consciously or unconsciously, tried to construe a rigid pattern
in which all civilizations had to fit, developing as they did in his
idea according to inescapable laws like an organic being. Toynbee, on the contrary, proceeded along the tested British path of
empiricism, without—or at least intending to be without—preconceived ideas. Spengler, therefore, is a determinist; Toynbee
is—or at least means to be—an empiricist. Spengler's view implies the predestination of all civilizations; Toynbee believes in
the free choice of each civilization, just as well as of each individual, to determine its own future. In Spengler's view all civilizations must inevitably follow one specific course; in Toynbee's
there is an endless variety of possibilities, although certain long-
range lines of development can be construed from the similarities
between them. In this respect Toynbee is supported by nearly
all other authors, who often consider even his pattern too rigid.

Such a fundamentl difference of views had to lead to different
conclusions about our own times. In Spengler's view the knell has
sounded for Western civilization and the only choice remaining
us is that of undergoing our inevitable doom with more or with

less dignity, of dying as gentlemen or as cowards. Toynbee's final view on this point still awaits expression, but from a number of his utterances we may take it that although the signs of the times fill him with great concern, he does not hold the fate of our civilization sealed. That, certainly, is the view of most other authors.

With the possible exception of Spengler, all the writers agree that the great crisis of our age is not necessarily tantamount to the fatal last act in the drama of human history. In spite of its apocalyptic character, its further development can be stopped and eventually replaced by a new constructive era. [Sorokin, *op. cit.*, p. 319.]

But notwithstanding these deep-rooted differences in outlook, in national and spiritual basis, in method and approach, there nevertheless remains a striking similarity in the general conclusions at which Spengler, Toynbee and others have arrived.

This similarity is still more remarkable if we see, as has been pointed out in Chapter II, that much earlier another philosopher, claiming to belong to a different civilization and writing half a century before Spengler and Toynbee, arrived at very similar results.

THE CONSENSUS OF THE AUTHORS DISCUSSED

To begin with, all three authors, as well as many others, recognize under some name or other the fact of the birth or dawn or emergence of a civilization after a "historyless" era which knows only a purely ethnographic form of existence and no *living* civilization. This dawn of a civilization is its first or archaic time; characteristic of it are mythology, epic poems and primitive art; it is the epoch of the great bards and primitive masters. One philosophy or religion undisputedly rules the material, social and spiritual aspects of society; worldly and spiritual authority are combined or closely connected, and exercised by a theocratic-aristocratic upper class by means of sacral laws and ethics. Rigid moral standards are generally recognized; community life is dominated by strong family ties. The economy of this period is rural and agricultural; hence those who own the land, i.e., nobility and church, dominate both socially and economically.

The period of spring, or bloom, or youth, or rise, which follows is inaugurated by the birth of the towns. This event renders the human mind more independent from clerical and feudal strains, stimulates it to activity and thus generates an intensive intellectual life. Yet religion continues to prevail over nationalism, intuition over reason, tradition over utilitarianism, spiritual over material values. This implies a unity of inspiration and a corresponding sense of style which sets its seal on all those products of art, philosophy or politics for which each particular civilization is gifted. It is the "period of the great masters."*

However, the rise and growth of the towns gradually leads to a new phase, in which the city becomes entirely predominant over the countryside; its leading inhabitants, the commercial middle class, take over from the ruling group of ecclesiastical and rural nobility. The flourishing of spiritual activity in the towns, which brought about a renaissance of the human mind, gradually leads to its complete emancipation from religious discipline: spiritual life becomes secularized, the fine arts, law and ethics become independent from religion, their value becomes a subject of dispute and individual appreciation. Materialism starts to prevail over religion, utilitarian considerations over inner feeling, technique over genius. Science comes to the fore and brings about an increasing control both over the physical surroundings and over the human environment, in other words: improved technique and geographical extension of the area of domination of the civilization. But these phenomena are neither causes nor proof of an increasing strength of the civilization; according to Danilevsky and Toynbee they often even

*For a more elaborate enunciation of the characteristics of this phase as recognized by many authors see Sorokin, *op. cit.*, p. 293.

tend to hide the internal decay which has already set in with this phase of "summer" or "maturity."

The fundamental source of the decay does not, in the view of most authors, lie in external conditions, but in internal causes, notably in a loss of creative force, which is depicted by Spengler as a domination of intellect over instinct, and by Toynbee as a failure on the part of the leading creative minority in the society to devise adequate responses to particular challenges, causing a failure of the society to adapt itself to a changing situation. While there is a difference in accent and in explanation, there is on this point a common denominator between these two and many other philosophies.

The strongest similarity in views between most philosophers is noticeable with regard to the last phase, that in which disintegration finally occurs. (Danilevsky does not deal with the characteristics of this phase.)

Spengler mentions as typical phenomena of this period: prevalence of the world-city, the "megalopolis," marked by the reign of its inhabitant, the intellectual nomad, and of its main power, money; physical sterility, and, accompanying it, spiritual sterility, i.e., disappearance of creativeness, loss of "style"; finally, world peace, resulting from the existence of a virtual monopoly of power, a "world empire" in which national and ideological wars are ended, but replaced by "private wars" of the Caesars; and a second religiousness as reaction against the preceding supremacy of intellect.

Typical characteristics of the last phase indicated by Toynbee are: a time of troubles, followed by a universal state; an internal proletariat which seeks refuge in a universal church; and an external proletariat; the combined forces of the latter two finally bring about the visible collapse of the universal state and of the civilization of which it is the last embodiment, if the civilization proves unable to devise an adequate response to the challenge of the time.

It will be clear that, although expressed in different terms and tinged by a different vision, these two pictures of the last stage of a society present some striking resemblances: the period of great troubles, of large-scale wars between ever larger units, in which finally one wins out and imposes a universal peace and a universal state; the advent of dictators and demagogues; the loss of creative force; the loss of style, evident in an artistic "sense of promiscuity"; the refuge which the suffering and weary masses seek in world peace and in religion; finally the return of society to a primitive state without living civilization— all these are common traits in the picture of both authors, and of a number of others as well.

For the conclusions common to the main authors discussed are supported by the fact that others, on an entirely different basis, have reached the same findings. To mention only one example:

The Russian philosopher Berdyaev, although fundamentally in disagreement with the cyclical view of civilization, arrives at results which are in many respects a confirmation of the above. He discerns in our Western culture a Barbaric, a Medieval-Christian and a Humanist-Secular phase, followed by the "New Middle Ages." During the Middle Ages our civilization accumulated creative forces or "spiritual fission-forces," as he calls them, through the discipline of monkhood and knighthood, both concentrated upon the Kingdom of God. Thereupon humanism put man in the center of the universe, releasing his pent-up inner creative forces; it brought the unfettering of man from the superhuman controls, the secularization of life, the flare-up of artistic creativity. Having spent its creative force, our civilization is now entering into the phase of the "New Middle Ages," characterized by a lust for "the full real life," a desire for prosperity and happiness and the enjoyment of life which tends to strangle the self-effacing discipline required for creative activity.

Still other authors who do not accept the cyclical view of history discern in the stages of our or other civilizations many characteristics similar to the ones borne out in the preceding pages. (For an elaborate and impressive summary of these similarities in different philosophies see Sorokin, *op. cit.*, pp. 292-294.)

If three or more historians with such a wide knowledge of facts, of different nationalities, writing at different times, basing themselves on different philosophies and using different methods have come to conclusions presenting so many similarities, there must be a strong assumption in favor of their correctness.

This assumption finds confirmation in certain clear and generally acknowledged facts against which they can be tested by every thinking individual.

THE FACTS OF HISTORY

We speak of civilization*s* in the plural. This implies that there have been more civilizations than one in the course of history. It furthermore implies that civilizations are born and die, or at least appear and disappear. Whether they are born from a period without civilization and wholly die, as Danilevsky and Spengler say, or whether they withdraw into a cocoon of religion in order to re-emerge in the form of a new civilization, as Toynbee says, or whether some of their perennial values survive and are absorbed by later civilizations, as others contend, is largely a matter of words and of metaphor.

It is furthermore equally certain that a civilization does not remain static from the moment of its appearance until that of its disappearance. Each civilization at one (or sometimes more) stages reaches a height of bloom, which implies that there are one or more processes of growth leading up to it, and of decline following it.

It also seems undeniable that in each civilization the weight of economic and civilized activity has shifted from a primitive rural, agricultural community to the cities, and through them finally to the metropolis. Concurrently the hub of power in each society has shifted from the priesthood and the landowners (the feudal aristocracy) to the money-making class (the bourgeoisie), hence to the masses, and hence to the demagogues or Caesars. Hand in hand with this movement there has been a development in many civilizations toward ever larger political and economic units, from the counties and boroughs to the city-states, hence toward countries, which gradually combine into two or three mammoth states, and finally all come under the dominance of one power.

It is also a fact that in former civilizations the phase of the metropolis, the universal state, and the Caesars, although in some cases of very long duration and experiencing ups and downs, never lasted indefinitely, and must therefore be considered as the last act of the life drama of a civilization.

All the established facts mentioned here, and recognized under differing names by many eminent writers, plead strongly against the view that no general trend can be discerned in the life of different cultures, and against the thesis that history can at any moment at any stage turn in any direction.

Some broad general trend of development common to all civilizations seems undeniable. To say, however, that they are consequently all bound to follow one inflexible pattern is too far-reaching and rigid a conclusion, drawn from too close a comparison with physical organisms. Even in the life of man, beast and plant there are thousands of different possibilities.

There is no reason why there should not be at least as great a latitude of variety for a society as there is for an individual; on the contrary, it should be greater, since a society is not bound by the laws of *physical* development.

Yet, even for a civilization we must on the basis of historical evidence assume that retrogression is possible to a limited degree only. There have been no examples of a civilization which had reached the phase of the world-cities moving back to that of an agricultural primitive society unless through such a process of disintegration and degeneration that the civilization would be lost or entirely change its character. The development of civilizations, as of all life, can move upward or downward, never backward.

This possibility of wide variations on a broad basic theme is notably evident in the two phases which are of specific interest with regard to our time, i.e., that of the greatest development and the subsequent one of decay. Again let us look at the facts of history.*

Egypt attained a first peak in its civilization during the Third, Fourth and Fifth Dynasties, that is, between 2780 and 2420 B.C. This was the result of a long period of unification and internal peace which had lasted since about 3200 B.C. During the next four centuries the Nile valley experienced a weakening in the power of the Pharoahs, resulting in rivalry, local warfare, intrusion of a foreign race, and a noticeable decline in economic and cultural achievements. Around 2000 B.C. the Princes of Thebes re-established a well-ordered centralized government over Egypt. This so-called Middle Kingdom was maintained until 1788 B.C., and gave birth to a second flowering of Egyptian civilization as reflected in the beauty of its tombs and temples, its painting, sculpture and literature. Internal political and economic decay thereupon enabled the foreign tribe of the Hyksos to establish its reign over Egypt without a blow, which inaugurated a second dark age. Around 1500 B.C. the Egyptians succeeded in chasing the Hyksos and establishing a remarkable second comeback of their greatness in the New Empire under the Eighteenth Dynasty (until 1350 B.C.). Great temples like those of Luxor and Karnak and the tomb of Tutankhamen date from this third flowering of Egypt's civilization. After a renewed and prolonged dark age Egypt finally staged a brief rally in the Saitic Revival of the seventh century B.C.

*The following data are based, among other sources, on *The Rise and Fall of Civilization* by Shepard B. Clough (McGraw-Hill, 1951).

Thus it appears that Egypt knew at least three high tides of civilization, alternating with ebb tides and spread over a period of some 1,500 years. If one wishes to include the Saitic Revival there are even four peaks, stretched over 2,000 years.

In the same way Sumeric civilization knew two peaks, separated by a dark age under foreign domination. The first was a creation of King Sargon of Akkad in the twenty-fifth century B.C. The second, outshining the first in cultural achievements, occurred in the twenty-third century B.C. after the expulsion of the barbarian invaders from Gutium, and lasted until the beginning of the twenty-first century B.C. Thereafter the valley of the Euphrates and Tigris was invaded and ruled by foreign tribes of inferior civilization.

One of those, however, the Amorites, founded the First Babylonian Empire, which under Hammurabi (*circa* 1750 B.C.?) reached the height of its civilization, expressed among other things in a great literary revival and the compilation of a code of laws. Around 1650 it was in its turn ended by foreign invasions. However, some 1,000 years later, in 625 B.C., it performed a comeback in the Second Babylonian Empire, which for some hundred years brought a revival of creative activity and re-establishment of Babylon as the center of the world under Nebuchadnezzar II.

Assyria, too, had two great periods, one under the reign of Assurnazir-pal II (883-859 B.C.), and another one some 150 years later in the New or Second Assyrian Empire.

If one considers, as is usually done, Assyria and Babylonia as belonging to the same civilization, then this civilization had at least four apexes.

The Later or East Roman Empire, which can in a sense be regarded as an offshoot or extension of the Classic civilization, lasted for over 1,100 years. During that period it, too, knew its ups and downs. After a brilliant start under Constantine the Great (A.D. ± 300), it experienced a decline in power and culture in the fifth century, followed by a revival in the sixth, culminating in the reign of Justinian. In the seventh century a new decline occurred, but in the eighth and ninth reforms and good government brought the empire a new period of flowering, until in the middle of the eleventh century the final decline set in.

These examples suffice to draw some important conclusions.

One is that a civilization does not necessarily have to culminate in *one* peak: it may have two or more, and they may be far apart in time. Consequently Spengler's thesis that all stages of a civilization, including those of maturity and decay, have a specific predetermined and limited duration does not tally with the facts, since for Egypt the heights of its civilization stretched over 2,000 years, for Sumeria over 500 years, for Babylon over 1,500 years, and for Byzantium over 700 years.

Furthermore it is evident from the history of these societies that their periods of political, economic and cultural productiveness occurred when they were independent and united under a well-organized central government, whereas internal warfare and strife led to invasion by "barbarians," foreign tribes of inferior culture, who temporarily blotted out the civilization in question or destroyed it completely.

It follows equally from the examples quoted that, contrary to Toynbee's view, even the conquest and occupation of a "universal state" by barbarian warbands need by no means constitute an irrevocable end of the civilization it enshrines: surprising rallies have occurred, sometimes after centuries. Thus Egypt, Sumeria, Babylonia and Assyria all knew a New or Second Empire, sometimes even greater than the first. The most remarkable comebacks probably were those of Egypt under Ichnaton and of Babylon under Nebuchadnezzar the Great.

This leads to a further conclusion which emerges from the history of former societies: the influence which great leadership has exercised on their fate. Sometimes such leadership even seems to be the only cause of an otherwise unaccountable rally. That, no doubt, is a deceiving impression, because even a great leader can only bring to the fore forces that are latently present in a community. But their inspiration can nonetheless apparently be of immense consequence in history. This again contradicts the defeatist view of Spengler that man is but a powerless tool in the hands of destiny and has to undergo the fate which history has spelled out for him.

These conclusions do not vitiate the fundamental fact which has been shown to emerge both from some extensive scientific investigations and from the empirical analysis of generally known facts, that the life of civilizations presents at least some general broad trend of development, even though thousands of variations are possible upon it.

THE TEST OF DECAY: LOSS OF CREATIVITY

Having reached this conclusion, the next essential question to be answered is: what, on the basis of the foregoing, seems to be the quintessence of decay? Is there a test by which we can determine its presence, and perhaps even its degree?

It seems to us that there clearly is. All the phenomena of decline of a society, all the causes indicated as its original source, have one essential in common: a loss of creative power. Whether one attributes the breakdown of a society to a failure to devise an adequate response to a challenge, or to a failure of the dominant minority to retain the voluntary allegiance of the masses, or to a vanishing sense of style, or to a replacement of instinct by reason, the essence always is a loss of creative capacity.

This is also the root of all such aspects of decline as: the replacement of great ideas and principles by personal strife as motivating factors in public life; the absence of new great styles in art; the absence of new philosophies, with the exception of the universal church—which, however, is already no longer of the old civilization; the loss of sense of style; the increasingly intellectual character of spiritual life, followed by a movement away from rationalism; the decrease of dynamics and vigor of the society *vis à vis* its surroundings; the physical sterility, with its sequence of depopulation. All these trends can be traced back to a decline in creativity, both physical and spiritual. Since they spring from a decline in creativity they can also be reversed by a revival of creativity.

The test for determining whether a society has gone into decline or not, therefore, becomes a matter of determining how strong its creative forces are.

Before we set out on the hazardous track of trying to apply that test to Western civilization, it seems necessary to estimate at what stage of the normal development of a society we stand.

PART II

The Present Phase of Western Civilization

VIII

Where Do We Stand?

WHEN we try to determine which phase of development Western civilization has reached it is easy first of all to indicate a few stages in which it does *not* find itself.

It is obvious that we are *not* in the early, archaic period of a primitive rural society with strong faith and stern style, in which each civilization finds its origin. Our civilization experienced that phase in the Middle Ages; it was in its medieval castles and, more still, in its cloisters, that the first sparks of Western civilization began to glow; it was in the songs of its minstrels, in its sparse Gothic furniture, in its primitive religious paintings and its mighty cathedrals, in its code of knightly conduct, in its stern Christian laws and moral prescripts, in the reign of Charlemagne, that our civilization found its first manifestations.

It is equally obvious that our civilization does not find itself in the subsequent period of growth, characterized by the birth and rise of the towns and the first blossoming of intellectual, artistic and commercial life. Western society passed through that phase in the time of the Renaissance and of the Revival of Learning, which constituted a declaration of independence of the human mind from the powers to which it had been subject in the Middle Ages. That movement blossomed forth when the universal grasp of the church and the feudal system upon society began to weaken, when the towns began to take the place of the castles and the cloisters, the burgher that of the feudal nobleman and the cleric, industry and commerce that of agriculture, when arts and sciences burst out with a profusion of rich blossom.

Our civilization must therefore find itself either in the subsequent period of maturity, or in the final stage of one civilization-wide controlling power, of universal peace and a universal church.

The gigantic military, economic, political, ideological, class and racial conflicts which our twentieth century is witnessing make it obvious that we have not yet reached the latter phase. At the same time, however, these very facts constitute, in the reading of history, the symptoms that that phase is near at hand.

Closer scrutiny of the symptoms of our time, however, is mandatory, before jumping to conclusions.

It is extremely difficult for any contemporary to assess in the right perspective the forces at work in his own time. It is difficult to avoid the natural inclination to overestimate the trends of the present, both in their favorable and unfavorable aspects, or to idealize and simplify the past. The period which has elapsed since World War II is obviously too short, in terms of the life span of a civilization, to permit the drawing of conclusions from it alone. If we wish to determine the characteristics of our present time we must draw into our survey a period of at least several decades.

Every starting point chosen for the analysis of a particular phase of history is to a certain extent arbitrary, since history is a continuous development which cannot be divided into neatly separated compartments; yet for purposes of method certain dates are often accepted as the beginning or end of a particular phase.

The most significant year, if one were to choose a specific year as marking the beginning of "our present time," is probably 1914. Most of the characteristics mentioned hereafter have either originated or become clearly visible after that ominous year. Yet many of them had been born or were in the making before then. Since it is not necessary in a survey of social developments to take a particular year as a starting point, it seems best to draw into our survey approximately the elapsed part of the twentieth century, and more especially the four decades since the outbreak of World War I.

THE CHARACTERISTICS OF OUR TIME

Development toward Larger Unities

From approximately the sixteenth century, when most of the national states of Europe took their present shape, until the beginning of the twentieth, the world scene was dominated by the interplay of forces between the most important of those states individually: Portugal, Spain, Sweden, the Netherlands, France, England, Russia, and, under successive names, shapes and regimes, Germany, and finally Italy, in succession or simultaneously played leading roles in which they could independently determine their fate. Sovereignty was a reality.

One of the most important facts of the twentieth century is that the national state is becoming obsolete. There is a clear development toward larger unities. This takes shape in the creation of universal organizations like the League of Nations and the United Nations, as well as in the growth of regional structures in the Arab world, the Latin-American world, the South and Southeast Asiatic world, Western Europe, the North Atlantic community, most of them welded together in political and economic organizations. These regional groups are more than the alliances of former times, which were merely temporary combinations of national states which could at will terminate their alliance and replace it by a different one. The unities that are now growing are functional communities whose political, economic, religious and cultural connections are slowly weaving them into an inextricable texture. The nineteenth-century sovereign national state is outmoded. We have arrived at a stage where the national states in whom power was vested before have been dwarfed by a few gigantic powers of almost continental size, which are now struggling for leadership in the world. It is undeniable that the ultimate decisions in the world of today emanate from only two or three centers and that the rest of the world can, when it comes to really important decisions, ill afford not to heed the wishes of those centers.

Economic conditions, too, have come to a stage where the average national state of the nineteenth century has become too small to survive; only mass production and mass consumption on a continental scale nowadays offer the possibility of economic survival and of improving the standard of living.

An Age of Great Wars and Conflicts

It is unfortunately all too clear that we are right in the midst of a "time of troubles," a "period of contending states," no matter whether this period started with the Napoleonic wars, as Spengler contended, or with World War I. The present century has already seen two wars of unsurpassed magnitude and destructiveness, and another one in Korea of considerable dimensions, and even if a third World War, of which there is so much talk, can be avoided, this seems sufficient to brand our time as one of great wars.

Furthermore our century has given birth to an ideological warfare which has no doubt had its equals in violence in earlier ages (Moslems against Christians; Protestants against Catholics), but not in the extent of its field of battle, which now encompasses the entire globe.

At the same time the first half of this century has witnessed the rise of nationalism in Asia, with all the violent antagonism against the white man, the conflicts, the strife and the bloodshed it has brought about, and which has finally resulted in the end of Western domination over Asia. One need only ponder the magnitude of this change and recall all the turmoil which has, starting with the Boxer rebellion, accompanied it in nearly all countries of Asia and in parts of Africa, to realize that in those continents, too, this has been a century of great conflicts. All this, therefore, more than justifies the application of the name "time of troubles" to the twentieth century.

Yearning for Peace

Under these circumstances it is small wonder that the hankering for world peace, the clamor for "one world," on the part of the masses, which are the sufferers of all this military, ideological and racial warfare, is growing stronger by the day. The longing for peace, ever alive in the hearts of men as a noble ideal, has swollen to a passionate cry for survival.

When the Tsar of Russia in 1899 took the initiative for the convocation of the First Peace Conference in The Hague, this marked the first attempt to transfer to the realm of practical politics the aim of lasting peace, which had up to then been regarded as little more than a pious ideal to which lip service had to be paid. Today the question: Shall we have peace or war? dominates the life of every man and every woman in all nations, and no government can afford not to put its striving for peace above all else whenever it is trying to obtain the support of the people.

The Age of the Masses

In the nineteenth century, the age of liberalism and of the Industrial Revolution, power was in the hands of the third estate, the bourgeoisie, the leaders in commerce and industry. In the twentieth it passed from them to the fourth estate, the masses. This century, as Ortega y Gasset has described, witnessed "the revolt of the masses." All signs, according to him, indicate "that the mass has decided to advance to the foreground of social life, to occupy the places, to use the instruments, and to enjoy the pleasures hitherto reserved to the few."

Our age is often called that of the common man. That is saying the same thing in different words. For the very essence of the mass is that it is made up of the common men, who constitute the immense majority of each nation or city or meeting, and to which usually you and I also belong, though we may not like to admit it.

This development has been caused by a number of factors.

The first of them is the tremendous increase of population almost everywhere. The population of Europe, for instance, from the sixth century until 1800 never exceeded 190 million; from 1800 to 1950, however, it grew from 187 to about 580 million. Still greater increases have occurred in parts of Asia and of the Western Hemisphere. And the figures which will be given further on in this chapter on the growth of some world-cities speak a still more eloquent language. If one ponders the extent and consequences of this fantastic increase it is not surprising that every place in the world where men are wont to gather, from the temples of Delhi to the restaurants of New York, seems permanently overcrowded and that according to a United Nations survey of social conditions there is no country in the world without a constant housing problem.

In addition to the increase in population these other factors have contributed to the rise to power of the masses:

The continuing expansion of the Industrial Revolution with the ever-growing labor class it created,

The consequent rise of the labor unions, a process which is only in its beginning stage in Asia,

The revolutionary development of the means of mass communication, particularly the newspaper, the popular magazine, radio and television, means which on the one hand brought the common man in direct contact with events the world over, and on the other hand made it possible to influence and control far greater numbers of people than had ever been possible before. In the United States it is possible today for an effective speaker to exercise his influence on some ten million people at a time over television, and to several times that number over the radio. The effect of this development is bound to grow much stronger still, both in the United States, where more than fifty-three million television sets are expected to be in operation by 1960, and in other countries, where the commercial application of television has only just been getting under way.

The outer evidence of the victory of the masses was the adoption after a process of gradual extension of the right to vote, of the universal suffrage by most Western countries in the twentieth century. The adaptation to this revolutionary change which made the acquirement of the mass vote the main object of politics has caused profound changes in the political life of all Western nations.

Since we are here only trying to determine the phase through which our society is passing there is no point in trying to appraise the gain or loss inherent in these developments. What matters is that the ascendancy of the masses is an undeniable sign of our time.

Hero Worship

But already there are symptoms that history is moving on to accomplish the eternal circle sketched two thousand years ago by Polybius: from monarchy (single-headed government) to aristocracy (government of the few), hence to democracy (government of the people), and hence back to single-headed rule.

This latter transformation has by no means taken place in all countries, but fertile soil for it is provided by the present-day hero worship found in differing degrees in almost all countries. This hero worship has in our days taken on unparalleled proportions, which in some forms are disconcerting because such hero worship has in the past often been the first step of the people toward abdication of their power in favor of one of their idols.

It is the irony of history that whenever the common people have after a long struggle obtained the power they have been striving for, they forthwith proceed to hand it over, in fact if not in form, to "strong men," public favorites who have for one reason or another attracted public support. Often the people instinctively choose the right man; sometimes, unfortunately, their choice is determined by emotional criteria irrelevant to the hero's capacity for ruling, and they find too late that they have picked the wrong man and now cannot get rid of him as easily as they adopted him.

The most dangerous form of this hero worship is, of course, found in the totalitarian movements. This is the most dangerous form because once the "strong man" is installed in power he cannot be unseated except at the price of a revolution, and often even an international war, with all the suffering for millions which these "remedies" imply.

Democracies, on their part, are by no means immune to hero worship, but with them it usually takes the harmless form of mass adoration of prize fighters, soccer or baseball players or movie stars. Sometimes, though, with them too it may take a less innocent turn when it reverts on purely emotional grounds to war heroes or to demagogues who have nothing to offer but their constant decrying of others.

The Rise of the Tycoons

Closely connected with the two last-mentioned phenomena of our time—predominance of the masses and hero worship—is the rise of the tycoons. They appear in politics, in the labor movement, in finance (though in that field their greatest era has passed), in business, in industry, in government administration. All these giants are successful because of certain qualities of skill, will power, perseverance, shrewd judgment, etc. These are, however, no special mark of our time. What has given these individuals the chance to build up such encompassing power in our day is the unprecedented magnitude of the machinery and the complexity of the problems involved. Both rendered necessary a unique concentration of power in the hands of exceptionally capable organizers. The common man, whether voter or member of a labor union or stockholder, realized that the job to be done is beyond his comprehension and capacity and is therefore often only too happy to leave the day-to-day management to its leaders. From the democratic point of view there are great advantages and no dangers in this as long as the *ultimate* power really remains with the people. It becomes a definite danger, however, if the ultimate power passes on to the leaders, and the people become mere tools in their hands, a danger which in politics is further enlarged by mass democracy's inherent tendency toward hero worship. It is one of the challenges of democracy in our time to find the right balance between on the one hand giving to the leaders in all realms enough power to enable them to do an efficient job, and on the other hand not giving them so much as to corrupt them or vitiate the minority right of dissent.

Declining Power of Money

In mentioning the rise of the great leaders in different areas of government and business we mentioned one exception: finance. The circumstances under which a J. P. Morgan, an Andrew Mellon or an Ivar Krueger acquired his fabulous fortune have apparently been on the wane for several decades. This is symptomatic of the diminishing role of money in Western society in many respects. Not that money is sought after with less avidity than before, not that it has become less convenient to those who possess it, not that it cannot still achieve a lot of things. What seems undeniable, though, is that the power and role of private capital has been on the decline for a considerable time.

International movement of private capital across all but a few frontiers has become virtually impossible or subjected to severe government restrictions, thus eliminating what less than fifty years ago constituted the main activity of international banking.

In domestic economy, too, private credit operations, though less hampered than in their international role, have in all Western countries become subject to many government restrictions.

Concurrent with these developments the governments themselves have taken an increasingly active part in both national and international financial operations.

All this, combined with the extension of the vote and the increasing publicity in which government is conducted in all democratic countries, has diminished the possibility for great financiers to play the part in banking and credit they used to before World War I; the influence of the great bankers on government, always overestimated by the outside world, has well-nigh shrunk to zero.

Furthermore taxes, increased to ten or twenty times what they were in the last century, have rendered the creation and operation of large private capital far more difficult than in the heyday of the Rothschilds or the Morgans. Inflation has reduced the value of national currencies in the most favorable cases to well under half what it was at the beginning of the century, and in the most unfavorable cases to zero or to a fraction of one percent.

Finally the scarcity of raw materials, consumer goods and housing in many Western countries has led to the imposition of limitations on distribution which have to a certain extent eliminated the power of money to buy material goods. The once unhampered play of the law of demand and supply has in the economy of most Western countries been drastically curtailed. Thus with the era of international free trade has ended that of the great international bankers.

It is outside the scope of this study to hail or bemoan this development; what matters here is its significance as a trend of Western society in our day, a trend which corresponds to one of the characteristics given by Spengler of the last phase of civilization.

The Growth of the World-Cities

It has been mentioned that the growth of a few enormous world-cities which make all the rest of the world seem provincial is another of the symptoms of the last phase of former civilizations. In our society that process set in during the nineteenth century and has gained momentum in the twentieth. To mention a few conspicuous examples:

Between 1870 and 1950 the population of the metropolitan area of London increased from 4 to 9 million, of New York from 1 to 8 million, of Berlin from 800,000 to 4.5 million, of Moscow from 600,000 to 6 million, of Jakarta from less than 260,000 to 2.8 million.

The present-day megalopolis conforms undeniably to the picture which Spengler painted of these monsters, which with their irresistible charm suck in the millions that fall prey to their glittering spell. Whoever has stood at night at the edge of that lake in Central Park in which New York's skyscrapers double their million lights, or has from the steps of the Sacré Cœur watched Paris vying with the beauty of the star-studded sky, cannot but conclude that this is the incarnation of his prediction. This is Babylon, Nineveh, ancient Rome revived.

The same applies to their population: housed in enormous mass tenement buildings, the inhabitant of our modern megalopolis has lost all connection with and feeling for the soil and all that it stands for. The home, once a man's castle, constructed and intended for life, has in these cities become a place for sleeping and eating (living is hardly the word any more), one out of millions of more or less similar spaces, constantly decreasing in size and in individuality, into which people move temporarily until they change into another one which is more convenient because it offers more cupboard space, an extra bathroom or a deep freeze.

The intellectual nomad has come to life.

Declining Birth Rate

A declining birth rate is another element which our time has in common with the last phase of former cultures. According to the *Encyclopaedia Britannica* "birth rates have been declining rapidly since the last quarter of the nineteenth century in practically all important countries of the world." It is not possible to verify whether this also applies in countries like Russia and China for which no reliable statistics are available. For most of the Western countries the trend is, however, evident from the facts. Thus the crude birth rate in England and Wales declined from around 35 per 1,000 in the period 1850-1880 to around 15 per 1,000 in the decade 1930-1940; in Germany the decline was from over 35 to around 17-18 per 1,000; in France from around 26 to 15; in the United States from 25.1 in 1915 (the earliest year of record) to around 17 in the years before World War II.

All these countries showed a marked rebound immediately after the war, i.e., in 1946 and 1947, but that was obviously a temporary phenomenon, similar to the one that manifested itself after World War I. What is more interesting, is that, contrary to what happened subsequently after that war, the birth rate in several Western countries at present seems to be settling at a slightly higher level than before the war. In 1948, '49 and '50 it was fairly constant in England and Wales at approximately 17 (against 15 prewar), in France at 22-21 (against 15 prewar), in the United States at 24 (against 17 prewar). It is too early yet to judge whether this is a permanent trend which reflects a rise both in physical health and in moral faith in the Western world.

Return from Rationalism

In the spiritual field, too, our civilization has developed according to pattern.

It found its birth in the Middle Ages in an art and philosophy, a political and economic system which were dominated by the church. Around the beginning of the sixteenth century the human mind started to free itself from the restraining influences of the church and the feudal system and entered an era of great enterprise and creativity. This generated the Reformation, the Renaissance, the Revival of Learning, Humanism, the world explorers. Yet the fundamental validity of the Christian religion was not challenged.

As the human spirit became ever more independent and bolder that changed in the course of the eighteenth century. It was then that for the first time the Christian faith itself began to be openly and publicly attacked. Earlier that faith had given rise to violent disputes and bloody wars, but those were only differences of church and sect, of doctrine and dogma. Now the value of Christ's teachings, nay the very existence of God, began to be denied. The seeds of this movement were sown in the minds of men in the eighteenth century by authors like Voltaire, the Encyclopedists and similar philosophers; its first harvest was reaped in the French revolution, its full fruit in the course of the nineteenth century: the Age of Reason had arrived. This corresponded to the usual third phase of a civilization, in which the process of secularization of spiritual, artistic and scientific life is completed.

But even in that same time the first doubts set in, and in the first half of the twentieth century the belief in the unlimited blessings of knowledge as a panacea for all ills of the world was well on the wane. Western civilization had by then in the course of some 400 years gone through the same experience and learned the same lesson which man usually learns in about four decades of his life: the emancipation from the domination of extraneous powers at first gave birth to a prolific upsurge of spiritual and artistic creativity, dominated by feeling, then was gradually replaced by an even more powerful development of mind with its products of knowledge and reason, science and technique— only to find in the end that all that in itself does not bring happiness: that brains are of little avail without character, that the staggering achievements of man's knowledge had not brought about the expected utopia. They had, on the contrary, entailed greater problems, greater conflicts, greater troubles. The Industrial Revolution generated the labor problem and the class struggle. Science, unfettered from moral restraints, increased human control over the forces of nature beyond all imagination, greatly enhancing man's comfort, prosperity, health and security. But at the same time it called into being forces of destruction to the degree where one bomb could kill 78,000 people and where future weapons may be able to wipe out civilized life itself.

Is it any wonder that in the twentieth century the people found themselves no longer satisfied by the state of affairs created by the supremacy of reason, or with the certainty it can offer for the solution of the troubles of our time? The Age of Reason is fading away.

Seeking refuge in other values, the people turn from the rational to the irrational. This turning away from reason can be traced in religion, in art, in science, in politics. Roughly speaking it seeks a solution in either of two directions: upward, in values higher than Reason, or downward, in values closer to earth than Reason.

Upward it seeks salvation in religious, philosophical, metaphysical or mythical solutions. A revival of religious interest and needs is noticeable in a number of countries. In the United States the percentage of the population which is affiliated with a church stands at an all-time high. At the same time the success in many Western countries of nonsectarian movements such as the "Oxford group" or "Movement for Moral Rearmament" is typical of the intellectual disappointment and spiritual hunger of our age.

In theology a significant development of our time is the success of neo-orthodoxy, which holds that man's fundamental questions about his existence can only be answered by faith, not by reason. Originated in Europe by Karl Barth and Emil Brunner it has by the middle of the century also achieved a strong influence in Britain and the United States (Dr. Reinhold Niebuhr) and seems to be still gaining in strength. (See *Awakening, The World at Mid-Century*, by Erwin Canham, pp. 182 and 184.)

Other utterances of this turning away from reason can be found in the many new creeds and "isms" which are vying for popular favor, cocktails made up of varying combinations of emotional sentiment, religion and pseudo-philosophy.

It would not be surprising if this urge toward the irrational were in future to find its apotheosis in a "second religiousness" and a universal church. Already the ecumenical movement has for decades been growing in the Protestant churches; already the once violent enmity between Catholics and Protestants is making place for co-operation in the face of the rising challenge of an atheist creed aspiring to take the church's place in fulfilling man's spiritual needs. It is therefore not surprising that in a speech in Edinburgh Toynbee predicted that the nineteenth-century movement in the Western world which replaced religion by technology as the center of interest will be reversed in the twenty-first century by a counter-movement in which mankind will turn back from technology to religion.

In art the movement away from reason and reality has found expression in different fashions that have come to the fore since World War I: cubism, futurism, symbolism, expressionism, and, most typical in this respect, surrealism.

In science the same trend is noticeable. "The physical sciences, which once challenged religion, now tend to support a metaphysical rather than a materialistic explanation of the universe and man." (*Ibid*, p. 178). Similarly in medicine the influential school of "psychosomatic medicine" proclaims that maybe as much as two-thirds of all human illnesses are a result of emotional conflicts and therefore not diseases of the body but of the mind or soul, and should be treated as such.

Even in politics the realization that a society cannot be governed by pure reason has become more and more apparent. The religious embodiment of this trend can be noticed in the democratic-Christian middle-of-the-road parties which came to power in France, Germany, Italy and other European countries after World War II.

The other, "downward" course taken by the anti-intellectual disappointment of our age is to deny all force higher than man and turn to the worship of purely earthly values. It may then take the form of hero worship, the deification of dictators or generals, of which we spoke before. It can also be recognized in the political fanaticism and the state worship which have swept the Western world since World War I and have by no means disappeared yet. Or it may crystallize in a materialist philosophy like historic materialism, or in a philosophy of "existentialism." Or it may simply apply the latter philosophy in its crudest material form: pursuit of prosperity and power, satisfaction of the senses.

Loosened Moral Standards

The spiritual evolution which Western civilization has gone through in the course of its existence has brought with it a corresponding evolution in the moral standards of society.

As long as spiritual and social life were dominated by religion, moral standards were part of it. Thus they bore the character of commandments of superhuman origin, absolute and beyond dispute. When, however, the human mind began to be emancipated and spiritual and social life became secularized, moral standards inevitably lost their absolute and superhuman character and assumed the nature of rules devised by men for the good of society. Thus utility and reasoned judgment replaced the divine will as their origin; instead of a godly command of absolute character they became a subject of human reasoning and speculation, subsequently of dispute, then of personal judgment, until finally their value came to be questioned altogether.

Two strong influences have furthered this process since the middle of the last century.

Historic materialism, by proclaiming economic factors as the origin of all developments in society, inevitably degraded moral standards to a mere function of economic factors.

Likewise Freudian psychology, by proclaiming the priority of sexual motives over all others, relegated moral standards to the role of a mere function of sexual factors.

On top of these movements in the field of thought, which had been at work for a considerable time at the outbreak of World War I, came the physical confusion caused by the world wars, the loosening of social standards of conduct and of family ties which we have witnessed since.

All this has resulted in a society in which the trammels of convention of earlier ages have been slackened and replaced by the loosely-knotted ties of utility and personal judgment. The attitude of the individual toward society, which once found expression in a rigid set of stringent duties, has more and more become a cumulation of rights, claims and demands; it has evolved from the Ten *Commandments* to the Declaration of Human *Rights*. This change in emphasis from duties to rights is not accidental; it is the natural result of the mentality of *carpe diem,* enjoyment, getting as much as possible out of life, which is rampant nowadays.

Loss of Sense of Style

One of the marks of recognition of a living civilization is that each of its periods brings forth a style of its own which is representative of that period and permeates all its aesthetic expressions. Western civilization has known a succession of such styles: Romanesque, Gothic, Renaissance, Baroque, Rococo. Huizinga has pointed out that the eighteenth century has up to now been the last to produce a homogeneous and harmonious style of its own. The nineteenth century no longer had a style, only a weak afterglow; its earmark is the lack of style, the mixture of styles, the imitation of styles. (Huizinga, *In de Schaduwen van Morgen,* p. 195.)

This loss of style, or "sense of promiscuity" as Toynbee calls it, is most easily noticeable in that form of art which has always had the closest connection with daily life and therefore been most representative of great periods: architecture.

Paris, probably the most beautiful city history has known, already showed the first signs of imitation of former styles in two of its most famous churches, built in the nineteenth century: one was constructed in the shape of a Roman temple and the other in Romanesque-Byzantine style. A still more remarkable collection of styles—which does not reflect on their beauty or national value—can be found in Washington, D. C., one of the capitals of the present world-wide civilization, where one can in the course of a short stroll successively pass public buildings and monuments in the shape of Greek temples, an Egyptian obelisk, a neo-classic museum, neo-classic, baroque and ultra-modern government departments, a Gothic hotel, and finally something which looks like the result of an intimacy between an Egyptian pyramid at ripe age and a Greek temple.

It must immediately be added that most of these and similar displays of a lack of style date from the nineteenth or very early twentieth century, and that architecture, as will be noted in Chapter X, is the very art in which our century has seen the birth of a strong new style.

Other manifestations of modern art, though by no means all,

show characteristics to which this description given by Sorokin
of the average phase of overripening seems singularly applicable:

> We find skilled technique which can reproduce anything but, having
> no strong soul of its own, it mixes all kinds of styles incongruously and
> conscientiously imitates the "primitive" style. Not idealism but sensory or
> visual naturalism is now supreme. Art is down to earth. . . . It imitates
> sensate nature and empirical reality. It has a particular inclination to the
> reproduction of the negative, the macabre, the pathetic, the passionate, the
> prosaic, the picturesque, and the ugly phenomena of life. . . . Calm
> serenity is gone, and instead we have distorted figures, suffering, ugliness.
> Women, who figure little in the classical art, are one of the favorite sub-
> jects in this phase. They are now depicted "realistically," in terms of
> voluptuousness, sensuality, sexuality, seductiveness, and "prettiness." The
> spirit of a purely sensate Epicureanism is conspicuous.

The latter characteristic applies not only to art in the strict
sense, but still more to those elaborate walks of life embraced by
mass entertainment and commercial art. We do not contend that
sex plays a greater part in modern life than it has done since
Adam met Eve; nor do we want to discuss whether it is a good
or a bad thing that much hypocrisy which used to cover that
subject has gone. What is, however, certainly significant for our
time, and is a sign of the "sensate" period of each civilization, is
that the alluring, provocative aspects of sex are today more
openly and more frequently depicted than in former ages. A
glance at any magazine rack or a page of movie advertisements in
any big city nowadays will suffice to bear out this statement.

Territorial Contraction of Western Civilization

At about the turn of the century our civilization had reached
the maximum of its territorial expansion. The last maiden ground
on the globe, the North and South Poles, had by then been discovered and thus the entire world was laid open to the influence
of Western economy, technique and culture. Not only the Western
world in its more limited sense, but also Russia, Asia and Africa
were under the domination of Western civilization in some form

or another, be it political or economic rule, commercial influence, technique, social habits, dress or religion. It often constituted only a very thin veneer at the top of society, which in many areas has since come off; yet at the time it nevertheless was considered the *ne plus ultra* even in non-Western societies. In this extension to the limits of the contemporary world Western civilization fulfilled another of Danilevsky's and Toynbee's criteria for the maturity of a civilization.

Since then the area of Western domination has contracted with a rapidity and to a degree which the West has hardly had time to realize yet.

In Russia and China some 800 million people now live under a Communist regime, barred from all the fundamental values in life that Western civilization stands for. Soon this one-third of the earth's population will no longer know, even from memory, what human liberty, democracy, freedom of speech, of press, of thought, of religion really mean; they will only know the perverted caricatures of these words which an efficient propaganda machine has branded into their mind.

In the rest of Asia almost an equal number have put an end to Western rule and become independent and in their resentment of a cast-off political domination may also repudiate values which they mistakenly consider as inseparably bound up with that domination.

It would be rash to conclude that the influence of Western civilization has diminished in proportion to its territorial contraction. For what it has lost in political control by the old colonial powers, it has on the other hand partly regained by the increase of American influence since World War II. Also it may well be that if the new forms of economic co-operation between advanced and underdeveloped countries now being worked out through Point Four and technical assistance programs prove satisfactory, newly discovered economic aspects of Western civilization may assume a new significance throughout these areas. In fact, as will be made clear in the next chapter, one of the great tests of our civilization is whether it will be able to meet the challenge of anti-Western nationalism.

Conclusion

As will be clear from Part I of this study, nearly all of the developments mentioned in this chapter have also occurred in other civilizations. They indicate that the third phase, that of maturity, has come to an end. On the other hand they show that our civilization has not yet entered the final phase, that of one universal power, universal peace and a universal church.

At the same time the crisis of our civilization finds expression in a number of challenges which point to the same conclusion, but which in view of their vital importance for the survival of our civilization deserve separate scrutiny in the next chapter.

It is most likely, then, that Western civilization is in a phase of transition from the period of maturity to that of civilization-wide peace; in other words it is in what Danilevsky considers the "post-civilization state of contradictions and conflicts," in what Spengler calls the first part of the fourth period, the "epoch of the Caesars," and in what Toynbee calls the "time of troubles."

Though the signs mentioned suggest the approach of its final stage, there is no reason whatsoever why they should imply the imminent end of our civilization. That was a conclusion drawn by Spengler's militarist mind, which reasoned: no fighting, no civilization. Both the duration and the cultural value of the coming last phase depend upon ourselves. If, with Huizinga, one considers the first century before and after Christ's birth as the zenith of Roman civilization, then we have hardly even entered the comparable and therefore greatest time of our civilization.

Neither is the duration of that last phase determined; it may last four or five hundred years, as it did in Rome, or it may last two thousand years, as it did in Egypt. It may constitute an era of decay and corruption, as in the last centuries of the

Roman Empire; it may also be an era which shines as an example of prosperity, beneficent administration and great art and learning as in the time of Augustus, in Alexandria and in Byzantium.

No civilization can move backward, but it has the free choice of moving either upward or downward. No civilization has been known to retrace its steps to an earlier stage; but many have been known to rise by the determined will of its peoples and rulers, or to fall by the absence of such will.

It is up to us.

IX

The Three Main Challenges to Western Civilization

IN THE preceding chapter we have pointed out a number of characteristics of our time which indicate that Western society is in a state of transition. Some imply shortcomings and weaknesses which could prove dangerous to our civilization. What renders its situation critical, however, is that in addition to these it finds itself confronted by a number of fundamental challenges, each of which could, if not overcome, be sufficient to spell its end. In this sense it is by no means exaggerated to apply to the present state of the Western world the much abused term of "crisis": a decisive development the outcome of which is to be survival or death.

The vital dangers to Western civilization are three in number. Like the characteristics discussed in the preceding chapter, they conform to precedent and pattern and tend to strengthen the conclusion reached there, that our civilization is approaching the phase of civilization-wide peace.

The first danger derives from an internal weakness similar to that of Greece in the fifth century B.C.; it is the disunity of Europe.

The second is the danger that peoples outside having wrested free from the domination of Western civilization may turn antagonistic to it; it is the anti-Western slant in the awakened nationalism of formerly dependent peoples.

The third challenge derives from a force which originated within our own society and could therefore be identified with an "internal proletariat," but which is at present at work inside as well as outside the Western world and has become largely identical with the system and interests of Soviet Russia; its name is communism.

COMMUNISM AND ANTI-WESTERN NATIONALISM

Both Russian communism and the anti-Western nationalism of formerly dependent areas have risen in revolt against what they considered domination of the world by the West and are now defying its leadership. Of the two, communism is thus far the more serious threat, since it aims directly at the roots of the political and economic system of Western democracy, erecting in its stead the idol of a political and economic system of its own. The anti-Western nationalism, though it has made its influence felt earlier and over a more extended area, seems as yet less serious a menace to Western civilization as such, because it has up to now directed its efforts mainly toward the limited aim of shaking off Western domination, yet retaining—as far as it has not come under communist domination—for the time being many of the political, economic and technical characteristics of modern Western society. No doubt Asian and other non-Western societies often have a strong and sometimes superior character of their own, especially in the cultural and spiritual sphere, but in our time they have so far not put forward any rival system which pretends to compete with both the democratic and communist systems. As long as this is the case the struggle is between these two, and the likelihood is that Asia and Africa will in the end adopt—and adapt—one of the two for their own needs.

Both Russian communism and Asian nationalism can perhaps be regarded as an "external proletariat" in the Toynbeean sense, in that they deem themselves underprivileged in comparison with the West; they are the "have-nots," and regard the Western nations as the "haves." (It seems regrettable that Toynbee should for the indication of these revolutionary forces have used the word "proletariat," which is usually identified with something inferior. In reality these forces are revolutionary counterforces, which need by no means be inferior or "proletarian." Where the word is nevertheless used in this book for these forces, this is done merely for the sake of indicating their identity with the Toynbeean phenomenon and not in a deprecatory sense to the movements concerned.) That the higher standard of living of the "haves" is due to their system of production, to the productiveness of their labor and to the inventiveness of their mind, is for comprehensible reasons not realized by the "have not" masses. They only see that the others are rich while they themselves are poor; hence they want to achieve the same prosperity, and if necessary reverse the roles. In such a situation nothing is easier than to whisper in the starved man's ear the venomous message: "Look how rich he is, and how poor you are. He got it by robbing you of your rightful part. Kill him, take his wealth, take his house, take his car and you will be the great man." This is the method which has been applied effectively by communism. It is only when the have-not acts in accordance with this insidious advice that he finds that he has murdered along with the "have" the secret of his prosperity. The real way for the "have-not" to be economically free and equal is not to murder the "haves" but to obtain the latter's secret and to apply it to his own circumstances. In other words to adopt and adapt for his own society the methods which will bring him similar prosperity. Only if Western civilization can hold forth ways which the East will recognize as best designed to achieve prosperity for itself is there a chance of the latter voluntarily adhering to these ways. The nationalism of underdeveloped areas could then very well lose its present anti-Western sting without in any way diminishing in national value. In order to achieve this, Western civilization must succeed in convincing these peoples of the universal value of religion and the freedom of man, which applies in the East as much as in the West.

In other words, there is no fundamental—as distinct from emotional—incompatibility between Western civilization and the nationalism of newly awakened nations; not only is their coexistence possible, but the closest co-operation between them is essential to a greater future for both of them.

The alternative is that communism may manage to bring the peoples of Asia and Africa into its camp, not only in the political or military sense, but—far more effective and dangerous—by instilling in them the conviction that only communism holds out the means toward a prosperous future. Then these masses, combined with those of the present communist world, counting altogether over fifteen hundred million human beings, would constitute an "external proletariat" presenting by far the greatest challenge which Western civilization has yet encountered. In addition this "external proletariat" would, under communist leadership, inevitably become allied with that part of the "internal proletariat" within the Western world, which has equally been brought under the direct or indirect control of communism. No civilization on earth has ever before been up against so wide and powerful a coalition from without and within as would then have been aligned under one leadership.

EUROPEAN DISUNITY

The crisis of Western society, like the crises of other societies in the past, stems not only from outside challenges like the two mentioned, but as much from one within. The latter resides in the division of Europe. The eclipse of European predominance in the political, economic and military field is, in the final analysis, due to its disunity. The internecine wars by which the old continent has been rent since the beginning of this century have temporarily bled it white. But even if those wars had not caused the *absolute* decrease in military, economic and political strength of Europe which in fact they brought about, its *relative* importance in all these fields would nevertheless have declined as a result of the process of the "dwarfing of Europe" by the greater national units emerging around it and overshadowing it, a process so suggestively described by Toynbee in his *Civilization on Trial*. The world wars merely precipitated this process and rendered the contrast with the previous European pre-eminence more conspicuous because it was encompassed by the memory of one generation.

The national units of Europe, with the exception of Russia, have simply become too small to play the role of "Great Powers" which they used to play in the world, or even to maintain a real political or economic independence. It may be argued that countries of the size and population of Russia, China, India and the United States have existed for centuries without impairing the leadership of the smaller European states. The explanation is that only present-day development of technique, communications, propaganda and mass government have enabled them to become really unified and to develop an economy and power commensurate with their size, resources and potentialities.

The eclipse of Europe in proportion to the rest of the world nowhere finds more eloquent and decisive expression than in the relative decline of its manufacturing capacity, a factor upon which political, economic and military power in the present world mainly depends. In 1870 England, France, Germany, Italy, Belgium and Sweden together produced 61 per cent of the world's manufactured goods; in 1936-1938, although their production had steadily increased in quantity, their share in the world's total had shrunk to less than 30 per cent. In the same period the share of the U.S. increased from 23.3 per cent to 32.2 per cent and that of Russia, which as late as 1913 was not more than 5.5 per cent rose to 18.5 per cent.

Only the reactionary can regret the rise of the non-European areas; they know of no better reply than to lament it, and would put the clock back—if their hands were stronger than those of the clock. They never are. If Europe really still has something to give, it can only prove so by performing the one reform which can restore it to its prominent role: integration.

There is no natural reason on earth why 300 million free Europeans endowed with a still unsurpassed intellectual genius and technical skill, possessing rich mineral resources and an immense industrial potential should not be able to regain a much greater position as one of the world's producers. Only the division of its economy into a dozen or more separate compartments stands in the way of the mass production and mass consumption necessary to boost European output to a higher share of the world's goods, which means: of the world's prosperity and power.

Whether Europe possesses the force to meet this challenge will be considered in the next chapter.

The challenges mentioned in this chapter, combined with the developments described in the previous one, tend to show that Western civilization is indeed on the threshold of what Danilevsky, Spengler and Toynbee would consider its fourth phase and that it is meeting the greatest challenge of its existence.

From this to deduct that our civilization is finished and doomed is a conclusion of unnecessary and unwarranted defeatism, which we must vigorously reject on the strength of what has been found in earlier chapters. That the phase of the universal state lacks greatness because it lacks international wars, is, as we have tried to show, a prejudice which could only spring from a militarist mind like Spengler's. That the "breakdown" which inaugurates the third phase of a civilization spells its inevitable downfall is a notion which we have found to be at variance both with Toynbee's own attitude toward predestination and with the examples he cites. There can be no doubt that the Augustan Empire did inaugurate the last phase of Roman civilization, yet it has been for centuries regarded as its peak, a shining example of a prosperous and well-governed state, the like of which is seldom found in history. Whether the Roman Empire and the New Egyptian Empire be considered as the Indian summer or as the apotheosis of their civilizations is largely a matter of words; their significance lies in their creative genius. And even in Toynbee's way of thinking there is no reason why that genius could not, at that late stage, still have produced an adequate answer to the challenge of their time and given a new upswing to civilization.

It is not within our power to turn the clock back to the rural society of the Middle Ages or to the early urban society of the Renaissance. It *is* within our power to make the coming final phase of our civilization the zenith of its dynamic and brilliant life performance, worthy of the most shining and valuable episodes that have existed in history.

There is no reason why even the tremendous challenge presented by the awakening of the underprivileged masses inside and outside the realm of Western civilization could not be overcome, given sufficient determination and vitality on the side of the West to do so. Whether the response is to be really successful is determined in the last resort not by a superiority in production, nor by a victory of arms, but by the inner creative strength of Western civilization, that is, its capacity to offer such spiritual, political and economic values to the world that even the underprivileged will voluntarily strive for them as the best means toward their spiritual and material welfare.

*   *   *

All that precedes, then, converges in this one conclusion: the future of Western civilization depends on the creative genius it will be able to show in meeting the challenges of our time. We are not doomed to a rapid fall, nor are we necessarily predestined to ascend to a yet higher culture encompassing the globe; the course of our civilization depends upon the forces within us.

If the last pronouncement is true it becomes all the more urgent to investigate the question mentioned before: How strong are the present creative forces in Western civilization?

It is a hazardous task to try to survey the world-wide field of present-day creative forces. The scope is really too wide to be encompassed by any one living mind; in addition the sources of scientific research upon which one can draw are smaller in number, and personal judgment is bound to play a much greater role than in examinations of the past. Nevertheless an answer to the question has to be attempted if we are determined to shape our own future on the basis of a realistic assessment of our fitness for survival. We shall, therefore, in the consciousness of inevitably falling short of the aim, try to take a bird's-eye view of the now living forces of our civilization. In doing so we shall again try to fit into our panorama as much as possible the pictures painted by others more expert in their field.

This author will furthermore draw upon the experience of a life in which it has been his privileged duty to live among some of the main nations of the West and keep a finger on their pulse: the French, the Germans, the British; the Dutch, the Belgians, the Danes; the Americans. His lack of knowledge of Latin America has forced him much to his regret to omit in this book any reference to that area which is playing an increasingly important part in Western civilization.

In surveying the forces of our civilization in the ensuing chapters no attempt will be made to pass a verdict of good or bad, beautiful or ugly. This is impossible for any contemporary and must be left to posterity. It is also unnecessary for the purpose of this book. The investigation must be limited to the question of how strong the creative forces are in our civilization; the capacity to produce fruit, not the taste of the fruit, is to be the object of our study.

X

The Creative Force of Europe

WHEN trying to gauge the creative force of Europe the most pressing question which calls for an answer is whether that cradle of Western civilization possesses sufficient vitality to conquer the main challenge threatening its future from within: its disunity.

CREATIVE FORCES IN EUROPEAN POLITICS

The amazing and hopeful thing is that it looks as if the old continent is really bringing up the creative force to achieve this well-nigh miracle.

In judging the progress made we must not measure with the yardstick of the American tourist, who is surprised and annoyed at the numerous frontiers he crosses and the endless formalities he has to submit to in traveling for a few hours through Europe. In order to achieve a balanced judgment we must measure with two yardsticks. One is that of the centuries that have led up to the present situation. It means that we must judge the progress made in the perspective of the seven hundred or eight hundred or thousand years in which the present nations of Europe have found their shape. Viewed in this light the advance achieved in the scant years since World War II has been astonishing. This statement may in itself seem astonishing to those who are irritated at the lack of visible results toward the unification of European parliaments, legislation, tariffs, production, armies, etc. Yet a summary of what has been achieved bears it out.

It will remain the historic merit of the Netherlands, Belgian and Luxemburg governments in exile in London during World War II to have laid the basis for the earliest and most far-reaching practical attempt at unification made thus far in Europe: the Benelux Economic Union. In its realization many obstacles have been met, some of which have not been overcome yet. But it remains the first concrete achievement since World War II toward economic and political integration of two countries which had for 350 years—with only one interruption of fifteen years— gone their own way.

The Western Union, concluded between France, Great Britain and the Benelux countries in 1948 is another such attempt. Its results have not been very tangible, and have been disappointing in the endeavor to build a common defense of Western Europe; yet, even if it should prove to have been nothing but a steppingstone toward the creation of the greater North Atlantic community, it remains of historic importance as one of the first tangible proofs of the will of Western Europe to strive for closer integration.

The next step, creation of the Council of Europe, was even more significant. Again, its visible achievements toward unification have been limited up to now. Yet it is of even greater importance than any of the other phenomena because it clearly sprang from the strong urge toward unification of the European nations themselves, inasfar as they could freely express their feelings. The Consultative Assembly, though limited to a consultative role, is a dynamic body which by its pressure exercises a real and constant influence upon the governments of Europe, whether they like it or not, to proceed faster upon the road toward integration.

The plan for a European Defense Community originally met

with many serious objections, and consequently was subject to many changes before it was adopted. But no one ever denied that it was an approach to the defense of Western Europe of a boldness and vision adequate to the magnitude of the problem. The same can be said about the North Atlantic Treaty Organization and its unified command for Europe. And finally the most difficult and most fundamental task has been undertaken: the creation of the European supranational authority, which will one day have to crown the integrated body of Europe. History only can show how far these endeavors will bring into being an adequate defense and an adequate unity of policy; what matters here to us is that drastic plans have come forth from European leaders and are being put into practice to meet the challenge of European disunion.

A united Europe would be of little value if it were brought about merely by pressure from the United States. On the contrary, it would then threaten to become merely an overseas province of the United States. The achievements mentioned, and the constant activity toward unification on the part of leading European statesmen like Briand, Churchill, Spaak, Stikker, Schumann, Monnet and Adenauer, are clear proof, if any were needed, of the urge of Europe itself for greater unity. This urge emerged as a living and dynamic force in European politics after World War II. A new Europe is in the process of birth. That is the clearest sign of the vitality of present-day Europe, and the strongest basis for the prospect that it will be able to respond successfully to its challenge.

In what forms this urge finally materializes is of secondary importance. Much of the machinery created has as yet been little productive; there still is too much sand and too little oil in the wheels and too little drive behind them. All that, however, is of later concern, as long as the process is rapid enough to meet the needs of the time.

This, we fear, is not yet the case.

This leads us to the second yardstick by which the progress of European integration has to be measured: its adequacy to solve the present problems of Europe.

Measured by this standard it seems undeniable that the progress made is still insufficient. Continuing at the present rate it would take some years before a unified European defense would be effected; and decades before a European market would exist of sufficient scope to enable European producers to compete successfully with those working for vast markets like the United States, India, Russia or China. This is too long to make certain that Europe will catch its breath before it is irremediably outdistanced by the mammoth powers around it. Time presses: if an adequate degree of integration should not be reached in time to prevent Western Europe from again being devastated by war and occupation, Western Europe will in future be admired for its history, its antiques and its ruins, but it will be out as a major factor in the world. It would then share the fate of Greece, which through its division fell prey to greater powers, successively Philip of Macedon, Alexander the Great, Rome, Byzantium. Even though its cultural radiation illuminated those mammoth powers for centuries after, Greece had ceased to count both as a world factor and as a creative source.

CREATIVE FORCES IN EUROPEAN ECONOMY

When World War II ended in Europe in May, 1945, the industrial production of the Marshall-plan countries of Europe had been reduced to almost half that of prewar. About seven years later, on the fourth anniversary of the European Recovery Plan, industrial production had in most countries of Western Europe increased to about 150 per cent of prewar, and agricultural production to 109 per cent. These very simple figures are the most eloquent answer to the question: how much vitality is there left in Europe's economic life?

This economic resurgence could not have been achieved without the stimulus provided by the Marshall Plan aid. It could still less have been achieved, however, without the necessary exertion and energy on the part of Europe itself, as is proven by the far less favorable results of similar aid in some other countries. The exertion of Europe even surpassed the expectation of the authors of the Marshall Plan in that a number of its goals were achieved in three years instead of four as anticipated. It seems a reasonable assumption that in many European countries the Marshall Plan's aim of restoring their economic balance by 1952 would have been achieved if the events in Korea had not completely unbalanced their terms of trade.

Yet, even making due allowance for the results of the Korean war, European economy as a whole obviously is by no means sound yet. Higher production alone does not provide a solution to the economic problems of Europe, deriving as these do from the fourfold source of war devastation, loss of overseas territories, increased industrial competition in other continents and the decrease of East-West trade in Europe. Only the creation of a single market encompassing, as a minimum, Western Europe, and the development of mass production can put Europe in a position to compete with other areas and to maintain and raise its standard of living.

"Functional" attempts at European economic integration are being made in several fields. Though they may not seem as spectacular and radical as one would like, each one in its field is an endeavor at an almost superhuman undertaking because it must radically reverse in a few years time what has grown in centuries.

Two such attempts have materialized up to now in the realm of economy, namely the European Payments Union and the Schumann Plan. The latter, particularly, welding together the steel and coal industries of France, Germany, Italy, the Netherlands, Belgium and Luxemburg, is a step of such historic significance that before World War II its materialization would have defied imagination. Combining far-reaching political and economic consequences, it thrust at what was the heart of European discord for at least a century: the rivalry between the French and German coal and steel industries. Great difficulties had to be solved, strong opposition to be overcome, cumbersome negotiations dragged on for a year—but the creative spirit of Europe won out. And already the next problem, that of Europe's agricultural integration has been tackled.

Thus in economics as in politics, though the progress made has been insufficient to achieve both the integration and the mass production needed, it can be concluded that Europe has shown sufficient recuperative power to recover its former prosperity and sufficient vitality to conceive of the methods necessary for the integration of Europe.

THE CREATIVE FORCE OF EUROPEAN ARCHITECTURE

Europe has shown itself capable of producing, in some fields of art, outstanding new forms or styles of lasting value. That this is so is particularly clear in three realms: architecture, films and music.

The rise of our civilization in the North Italian towns of the Renaissance was marked, among other things, by the emergence of a school of painting which has perhaps been equaled, but never surpassed. If one takes into consideration the small size of those towns, the number of great masters which they produced in a short time is truly astounding. It is these outbursts of creative force in a particular field which are the clearest sign of life of a civilization.

In the same way an entirely new style of architecture has sprung up in Europe in the first half of this century. From a maze of hitherto unco-ordinated lines and imitative themes, the straight line and the principle of functionalism emerged as the representative style of our time, bold of conception, a truly new creation and as strong an expression of vitality as the Doric or Gothic style was. Like any other style it has, of course, known its deformations and its excesses, but there can be no doubt that the modern quarters of Amsterdam, Stockholm, Berlin, Hamburg and many other European towns, and buildings like the town halls of Stockholm, Oslo and Hilversum will rank among the great creative achievements of Western culture. It is characteristic that they are not merely products of individual artists, made on individual orders; on the contrary, they find their most typical expression in the structures destined for mass use, such as office buildings, labor-class apartment buildings, factories, schools and public edifices, faithfully reflecting the supremacy of the masses. Neither has this new style petrified into the lifelessness of uninspired repetition: although it spread over the whole Western world as the "international style" of the twenties, it also branched out in the diversity of regional or group schools, such as the Amsterdam, Stockholm and Vienna schools.

If it is true, as Burckhardt has said, that the character of nations, cultures and epochs speaks through their architecture, then certainly the twentieth-century revival of European architecture is a most hopeful proof of its vigor.

CREATIVE FORCES IN EUROPEAN CINEMATOGRAPHY

Although the film is a more ephemeral form of art than others, it seems as important a test of the cultural force of our civilization, precisely because it is the most typical form of art and of mass enjoyment of our time.

No form of art requires such an accumulation of capital and material equipment as that mixture of art and technical production called the film industry. In both these two requirements European studios have been at a serious disadvantage compared with Hollywood. All the more remarkable is it that almost from the beginning several European film industries have consistently been turning out superior products.

It started right back in the early days of the silent film, when the Germans produced their first great masterwork the *Nibelungen*, followed by many other great creations until the day when the German film industry was forced into the Nazi strait-jacket and lost its originality. But already it is making its comeback.

The British film industry has steadfastly produced films on a high artistic level. Perhaps its most remarkable feat, however, is that during and after World War II, when both capital and human material were at a high premium, it succeeded in further raising its level and even capturing the interest of the American public. It not only turned out gems for the connoisseur, such as the Noel Coward and Somerset Maugham productions, but even big box-office successes—*Hamlet, The Red Shoes* and *Tales of Hoffmann.*

The same applies to many postwar Italian masterpieces which have had long runs in Europe and America, like *Open City, Shoeshine, The Bicycle Thief, Bitter Rice* and *Miracle in Milan.*

The French film, too, has reached unsurpassed levels of camera work, acting and direction. It has achieved such outstanding successes as *Carnet de Bal, Les Enfants du Paradis, Symphonie Pastorale, Le Diable au Corps* and *La Ronde.*

It must be added that both French and Italian postwar films are often pervaded by a realism, morosity, cynicism and lack of faith that are not exactly indicative of a healthy civilization. This does not, however, alter the fact that European film production, although lacking the financial and material resources, the guaranteed mass market and the talent at the disposal of Hollywood, has succeeded in turning out products of a higher standard and often unequaled creativity.

CREATIVE FORCES IN EUROPEAN MUSIC

In music it is more difficult to distinguish between the harvest of Europe and of America, since music is more subject to international influences. Its creators and interpreters have in the last decades moved between the two continents probably more than any other group of artists. Nevertheless, if the distinction is made, it is simply to test the cultural fecundity of the two cores of the Western world.

Scores of composers have come to the fore in Europe in the last decades: Milhaud and Poulenc in France, Honegger in Switzerland, Sibelius in Finland, Malipiero and Pizzetti in Italy, Vaughan Williams and Britten in England are only some of the more well-known names among them. Many others, born and educated in Europe, have worked in America: Paul Hindemith, Ernst Křenek, Igor Stravinsky, the late Arnold Schönberg and Bela Bartok. The mention of these names should be enough to demonstrate the vibrant creative activity of European music in the era of the World Wars.

In the execution of music, too—if that has any bearing on the degree of vitality of a civilization—Europe is still leading, as fertile as ever in the production of great soloists and conductors. Although the orchestras of Boston, New York and Philadelphia are probably unsurpassed anywhere, nearly all the great soloists and conductors today were born in Europe, including Russia.

This by no means implies that musical life is not flourishing in the United States, but it does indicate that most of the great creators and interpreters of music of our age were children of Europe and a proof of its cultural fertility.

XI

The Creative Force of America

TO ANYONE who knows the United States it must seem as superfluous to prove the vitality of the American people as it would be to prove that of a two-year-old bull. The pace, not only of its traffic, but of its everyday life, its dynamic and exuberant quality both as a nation and as individuals, the vehemence of its reactions and its feelings, the fantastic growth of its economic enterprises, the meteoric rise of its great men in private and public life, all these are so obvious even to the most superficial observer, that further investigation seems hardly necessary to anyone who has felt the pulse of American life.

But these outward appearances do not suffice for our purposes: they might deceive, they might merely be a sign of man's outward control over nature without the inner creative force to make it subservient to a special goal. Let us, therefore, look for fields in which the American mind is showing itself truly creative.

THE CREATIVE FORCE OF AMERICAN TECHNOLOGY

Born as an independent nation almost simultaneously with the steam engine, the life and growth of America have kept pace with those of the engine; its fabulous power and prosperity alike are in the last analysis dependent upon it; its influence is spreading over the world on the wheels of machinery.

It is in this field above all that America has shown a creative genius.

The United States [says the American author James Burnham] is mature in one field alone: in the development of the technique of production. In this Americans themselves do not understand their unparalleled supremacy. There is not, and has never been, anything approaching American methods of production. . . . It is not so much in the machines themselves, where England and Germany and perhaps Sweden and Switzerland have done better, that the specific United States superiority lies. It is rather in a talent, by now almost a national characteristic, for the large scale organization of production.

And he continues to point out that even in the development of the atomic bomb, for instance, almost none of the fundamental research was done by Americans, but that the true creative power of the United States expressed itself in setting up the tremendous process necessary for its production.

"Technological civilization" is regarded as an impossibility by those who consider technology the death of all civilization. This need not be: technological advance is as much a product of the human mind as scientific advance in other fields, and its application as dependent on human energy and ingenuity. Henry Ford's continuous assembly line, and its modern counterpart, the continuous-flow chemical plant, as well as millions of other small and large inventions which have gone into the modern processes of mass production, are as much creative utterances of the human mind and as much a contribution to civilization as the triangle of Pythagoras; their application has required no less purposeful planning and sustained energy than the building of the pyramids or the tower of Babel.

This is not to say that technological progress is the answer to all problems of the world, as some seem to think. Toynbee has pointed out that extension of control over the surroundings is in itself not a sign of growth in a civilization; on the contrary, it may tend to make man the servant instead of the master of his methods, and the technique an end in itself instead of a means to an end. But the point which interests us now is whether this vast agglomeration of inventions and processes and organization constitutes proof of a creative capacity in America. There the answer must be "yes" to anyone whose judgment is not predetermined by the deeply-rooted bias against "American materialism."

A system of production which has brought about the situation that a nation numbering 7 per cent of the world's population produces about one third of all goods and services, and is now aiding or supporting some sixty other nations is not to be underestimated as an achievement of human creative power and a contribution to civilization.

CREATIVE FORCES IN AMERICAN POLITICS

When searching for creative achievements in American politics it seems necessary to discard at the outset one notion which might occur to many Americans as a typical American achievement. The average American likes to think of democracy as an American invention. This it is not. Democracy as a system of government in which the ultimate power is derived from the will of the people is probably as old as organized society, but in our Western civilization it certainly goes back to a time long before Columbus crossed the Atlantic.

It cannot be said either that America has as yet developed a specific art of government of its own, such as the great contributions to civilization of Rome and Britain. This is not surprising since for a long time the main energy of the American nation has been devoted to the guarding of the frontier, the extension of the country and the exploitation of its immense resources. Until the 1930's government was considered in America only a necessary evil, a ring in which the economic competitors could try to knock each other out in a free-for-all fight. Only with the great depression did the art of government start to play the role in the United States which it had for some time played in other countries.

If, therefore, it cannot be said that America has either originated democracy as such or devoted itself specifically to the art of government, it would be short-sighted to conclude that the American people have not shown any creative capacity in the field of statecraft.

In this regard the most valuable American contribution lies not in the invention of any new principle or system, but in the successful application of two important systems, namely the federal and the democratic, to new circumstances and on a scale unknown before.

The Federal System

Though federal forms of government had been applied before in some European countries, these applications had remained within much smaller limits, both of space and of time. In the United States the system has now been in force for more than 160 years over an area the size of a continent and the principle is still as firmly rooted as ever in the American tradition, even though there has been a marked increase in the powers of the federal government.

To its application the United States owes many benefits. It has through a balanced distribution of delegated and retained powers rendered possible the efficient administration of a country three thousand miles wide, without destroying the direct interest of the individual citizen in his government and in public affairs. It has prevented domination of any one state by another or by the Union. It has rendered possible diversity within a sufficient degree of unity.

In our time, in which a growth toward larger unities is evident and in which a closer form of co-operation both in Europe and in the North Atlantic community is even a condition of survival for the West, these advantages of the federal system take on a new significance, since they seem well calculated to avoid a number of pitfalls ahead. This does not, however, necessarily mean that the system should in other cases be applied in exactly the same way as it is in the United States.

The Switch from Bourgeois Democracy to Mass Democracy

It is undeniable that there exists a certain difference between American democracy and that of the older West European democracies. It is this difference—not easy to define—which constitutes the specific American contribution to the cause of democracy. It can perhaps best be thus described: that America has succeeded in adapting democracy to the requirements of mass government.

Both the American and the French revolutions, although based on the principle that all men are born equal and entitled to life, liberty and the pursuit of happiness (*liberté, égalité, fraternité*), were not revolutions of the masses or of the common man. They were in the social sense essentially movements of and engendered by the propertied middle class, the *bourgeoisie*, the *tiers état*, the Virginia landowners, against an authoritarian government which did not allow them the say in public affairs to which they felt entitled. Only from the middle of the nineteenth century on did these political and economic rights gradually spread, often against the opposition of the bourgeoisie, to every man and woman, to the masses, to the "fourth estate" as it was sometimes called in Europe. It is in the successful extension from the limited eighteenth-century concept of democracy to the twentieth-century democracy of the common man that the true and specifically American contribution in the field of domestic politics lies. America has by way of a peaceful evolution, almost unnoticed, performed the revolutionary switch from *bourgeois* democracy to mass democracy, which communism achieved through the extermination of the bourgeois classes. Thus a system of government has, under retention of its name and fundamentals, been smoothly and successfully adapted to essentially changed conditions and requirements. The "challenge of new circumstances" has been met.

The close interest of the average American citizen in the public affairs of his country is achieved on the one hand through a system of education specifically aimed at this result, and on the other hand through the mass distribution of news and opinions on an unprecedented scale. American media of mass information devote a larger part of their attention than in most European countries to the task of commenting on and discussing the news in order to enable the general public to form a judgment. Nowhere do panels, forums, discussion groups, speeches at women's, garden, civic and businessmen's luncheon clubs, etc. play such an important part in public life as in America. Few European prejudices about America are as ill founded as the widespread notion that the American public is badly informed. The information it receives is perhaps less detailed than in Europe, but in no country is the general public so dragged into the important public issues, and in no country are these so extensively, exhaustively and violently debated.

One notable contribution which America has made in this field is the specifically American institution of the newspaper columnists, authoritative journalists who discuss public affairs in columns published daily by scores of newspapers, independently of the paper's own opinion.

Foreign Policy

In addition to these constructive contributions to the methods of mass democracy, the American nation has also given proof of vigor and inventiveness in the realm of foreign policy. This statement may seem surprising, since American foreign policy is one of the most beloved objects of criticism both from within and without.

In this respect we must emphasize once again that for the purpose of determining the vitality or decay of our civilization it is not the prudence of certain decisions or the delicacy of the methods that matters, but the dynamism, the adaptability to new circumstances, to which they bear witness. Even the most severe critic of American foreign policy will have to admit that these qualities have not been lacking since the United States in the 1930's started to give up isolationism and entered the arena of world politics.

The clearest evidence of adaptation is found if one simply looks back some fifteen years and remembers how the overwhelming majority of the American nation still clung to the maxim of "no foreign entanglements." Even Franklin Roosevelt, whom no one will accuse of isolationism, in the years 1934, 1935 and 1936, and even as late as 1939 and 1940 felt it necessary in his public utterances to hew to the line of nonentanglement, nonintervention and neutrality: "Your boys are not going to be sent into any foreign wars."

Today American soldiers, with the backing of the overwhelming majority of the nation, stand in Europe, in the Philippines, in Japan, in Korea. A more eloquent proof of the radical change that has taken place in the American attitude could not have been given. If anyone in America had predicted in 1935 that this would be American policy fifteen years later he would have been laughed at—if not worse.

Similarly, the main decisions of postwar American foreign policy: the Marshall aid to Europe; the Truman Doctrine for Greece and Turkey; the Berlin airlift; the Point Four program; the sudden decision to go to the aid of South Korea after the communist attack; the decision to integrate Germany in the defense of Europe—all bear the hallmark of initiative, courage and far-sightedness. Other nations, with longer experience and traditions, might perhaps have tried to achieve the same ends with more subtle means or greater patience, but that is not the point.

Equally the decisiveness with which the United States has

opposed communist expansion compares favorably with the wavering attempts to curb Nazi Germany in the thirties. So does the decision to resist aggression in Korea with the inactivity of the West toward aggresson in Manchuria in 1931 and in Ethiopia in 1935, and to the remilitarization of the Rhineland in 1937.

Altogether the characteristics of American policy since it has assumed a leading part in world politics are certainly not those of decadence, but rather those of youthful dynamism not yet restrained by experience and tradition.

Thus in politics, both domestic and foreign, America has given ample proof of that capacity to discern great issues and audacity to deal with them which have always characterized great nations and great civilizations at the peak of their vitality.

CREATIVE FORCES IN CONTEMPORARY AMERICAN ART

Until the fairly recent past the American nation's energy has been mainly absorbed by material problems: first the establishment of a white society in defiance of the Indians and of nature; then the conquering and development of the endless land mass unto the Pacific; then the feverish exploitation of its riches. It seems justified to say that as a result spiritual activity, particularly in religion and art, plays a smaller part, absorbs a smaller share of the national energy than in most European and Asiatic countries. The American mentality and pace of life are not conducive to the serenity required for either religious contemplation or artistic creativity.

Yet both the interest and the average productive quality in the fields of art have in the last decades been markedly in the ascent.

"If in arts and letters" says James Truslow Adams in *The Epic of America* "we have produced no men who may be claimed to rank with the masters of all time, we have produced a body of work without which the world would be poorer and which ranks high by contemporary world standards."

In drama, though not in all other forms of entertainment, America has strongly influenced the theater of the Western world by the quality of its playwrights, from Maxwell Anderson to Arthur Miller, from Robert Sherwood to Eugene O'Neill. In fiction authors like Sinclair Lewis, John Marquand, Ernest Hemingway, John Steinbeck, William Faulkner show a vigor and earthly warmth not indicative of decay: they are creating a literature well representative of special strata of present-day American society.

Musical life in the United States has reached a level equal to the best ever achieved elsewhere. Although the majority of the leading composers, soloists and conductors performing in the United States were brought over from Europe, the tremendous interest they are encountering and the perfection of their orchestras could only have been achieved in a highly responsive "climate," in a nation where the art of music is really alive. The ten symphony orchestras which the United States possessed in 1900 have by now increased to well over six hundred. Though these cannot all, of course, boast the quality of the Boston or Philadelphia, this growth in number is a sign of vitality of its musical life.

Still, neither American music nor drama nor literature, high as their standards are, constitute the strongest proof of America's creative faculties in the realm of the arts. The two fields in which it has, in our opinion, more important original creations to show are the film and architecture.

In mentioning a contribution in the cinematographic field we do not have in mind the "romantic claptrap" of which American film critics so often complain, but the serious endeavors made by a few producers to mirror in great artistic creations characteristics or problems of our time. Furthermore a new and typically American form of art has been created in the animated cartoon. To think of Walt Disney's creations as elements of Western civilization may cause many a highbrow eyebrow to be raised still higher. And yet, why should Popeye be less part of our culture than Tyll Enlenspiegel or le Maître Patelin were in their time, popular characters for public amusement in earlier centuries which are still being taught to European schoolchildren as evidence of early European civilization?

The lightheartedness of the cartoon film is not in itself a reason why it should not be a valuable contemporary contribution to the playful side which has never been absent in any civilization. Each time has its own forms of art for amusement, and the very fact that a period brings forth new and representative forms is the best proof of its cultural vitality. Only if America were today for the amusement of its masses turning out seventeenth-century pantomimes or nineteenth-century operettas, as some protagonists of "culture" would like to see, would there be real reason for concern.

This capacity to create new forms of art typical of our time has found its strongest expression in yet another field of art: architecture.

The name which immediately comes to mind in this realm is that of Frank Lloyd Wright, who as early as the first decade of this century introduced a revolutionary new style in building. For a number of years he found more followers and appreciation in Europe than in his own country, probably because of the lesser interest in architecture which existed at that time in America. Building usually was done in a hurry, efficiency and usability were more important than beauty and style. In America the use of an architect is even today still considered something of a luxury which can only be afforded for expensive projects.

This goes a long way to explain why the same nation which has erected so many large buildings of striking beauty and bold conception has at the same time allowed so many sections of its cities to be built without any style whatsoever or in a style of mediocrity and tastelessness.

Notwithstanding these handicaps the United States has given

birth to the man who became one of the main founders of a style of building which in our firm conviction is as important an artistic creation as the Gothic or Romanesque styles were.

In the first decades of this century the new style flowered and spread predominantly in Europe. The 1932 International Exhibition of Modern Architecture in New York aroused new interest in such outstanding European masters as Le Corbusier, Mies van der Rohe, Walter Gropius and J. J. P. Oud, as well as in the importance of Frank Lloyd Wright "at a time," to quote the Museum of Modern Art, "when most of the advanced Europeans considered him the exhausted founder of a mighty tradition, a romantic pioneer without place in the carefully calculated new architecture, and few Americans accorded him even the honor due a past master." The exhibition probably contributed to the new activity of Wright himself and to a new development in American architecture, in which the seemingly opposed idioms of Wright and Le Corbusier became amalgamated. Since then the creative activity of American architecture has expanded tremendously. Not all of it is of a beauty which will defy the ages. Many gaps remain to be filled. (It is surprising for instance, that on what could be one of America's finest avenues, Park Avenue in New York, the shape of most buildings, with the notable exception of Lever House, seems to have been determined exclusively by the municipal building ordinances. It is equally surprising that no aesthetic solution has been found yet for the elevator engine house on top of all American apartment buildings.) But a nation which can boast such creations as Rockefeller Center in New York, the Bronx-Whitestone, George Washington and San Francisco Bay bridges, the Veterans Administration Building in Detroit, the Watts Bar Steam Plant near Dayton, Tennessee, the Gateway Center in Pittsburgh and some of the new sections of Los Angeles, is certainly not in danger of relapsing into artistic sterility or creative impotence.

THE PROGRESS OF SCIENCE

The progress of science since the beginning of this century has been so stupendous that it is hard for mid-century Western man to realize how drastically it has changed the every day aspects of his life. Is it really less than sixty years ago that the first automobile slowly set itself in motion and the first airplane precariously took off from the ground for a risky few hundred yards?

Since the first horse appeared in the streets of Babylon until the invention of steam traction, i.e., for some four thousand years, man had known no faster means of transportation than the horse. For hardly a hundred years did he get time to adapt his life to the revolutionary changes of the steam engine. Then within a period of little more than fifty years science thrust upon him in rapid succession a series of inventions, each of which in its application was as incisive: the automobile, the airplane, radio, television, atomic energy, jet and rocket propulsion. All these were the result of the myriads of great and small achievements of physical science in which the twentieth century showed itself so fertile.

For hundreds of years the universe in which man was conscious of living had been encompassed between the scientific limits of the atom as the smallest indivisible particle of substance on the one hand and the stellar universe as the outer limit of known space on the other hand. Today science has shattered both these frontiers. Physical science has proven the atom to consist of a sort of stellar system of infinitesimal smallness; astronomy has shown the stellar universe to constitute only one of an endless number of galaxies, island universes in space; hence our galaxy constitutes in its turn only an atom in a substance of unimaginable proportions.

Western man stands reeling at the edge of this abyss of the infinite which twentieth-century science has disclosed before his eyes. The splitting of the atom constituted one of the most awe-some achievements ever performed by science, opening up a new immeasurable source of energy, of which we cannot nearly fore-see all the results yet.

But already Promethean man is bracing himself for new and more daring enterprises yet in order to break the shackles of his earthbound existence: science is seriously studying the possibility of such once-fantastic schemes as suspending a space ship above the earth, shooting space rockets to other planets, again doubling man's life span, artificially modifying the intellectual and moral characteristics of individuals and races.

Equally startling progress has been made in medicine, in chemical science, in biology, in psychology, in the social sciences, to mention only these. The achievements of Europe and Amer-ica in those fields are so closely interwoven that it is hardly possible to distinguish between the constructive part played by each of them. The most one can say is that scientific effort in Europe has been more directed toward fundamental and purely scientific research, in America more toward its practical applica-tion. Both have amply proven our century to be one of the most prolific yet in scientific achievement.

PART III

The Shape of Things to Come

XII

The Coming One World

IN THE first part of this book we have analyzed some of the
main philosophies about the lifecourse of civilizations and
have arrived at a synthesis of their main characteristics. In the
second part we have, on the basis of this general pattern of the
past, tried to determine what stage of development our Western
civilization has reached and to assess its present creative force.
This has led to the conclusion that our society is probably in the
throes of the upheavals which usually precede the period of world
peace, as Spengler calls it, or of the universal state, as Toynbee
calls it.

As far as the latter is concerned this view was confirmed by
Toynbee in his Edinburgh speech of October, 1952, in which
he predicted that "within half a century the whole face of the
planet will have been unified politically through the concentration of irresistible military power in some single set of hands."
Whether this unification will come about through a world war or
without it, he was unable to say.

But it is not necessary to draw on intricate philosophies of
history to come to the same conclusion. Measured by the
standard which in practice counts most, that of the speed of communications, the world has been shrinking at an increasing pace
with the advance of technology. In 1872 Jules Verne created a
sensation with his story of Phileas Fogg traveling around the

world in eighty days; nowadays one can easily do it in eight days; in a not too distant future, flying at supersonic speed, it may not take more than eight hours.

This fundamental change is profoundly influencing the structure of the community of Western nations, and, in fact, of the world. It is rapidly approaching the stage where it can no longer afford to have its left hand trying to cut off the right, since they have both become part of one body; to continue warfare on the scale of our present day would be like a bird pecking out its heart with its own beak.

The scope and intricateness of modern total warfare absorb such a disproportionate part of the national energy that no nation can support it for any considerable time without disastrous effects. The destructive power which the progress of technology has laid in the hands of man has reached the terrifying proportions where civilization can no longer afford to use it indefinitely for fighting and destroying parts of itself.

Also the exertion required by modern war has not only increased in proportion to the magnitude of total warfare; it has in addition been tripled by the sustained preparation it requires beforehand and the immense reconstruction it necessitates afterward.

Consequently the power not only to exterminate individuals, but mortally to wound an enemy nation and perhaps even extinguish its very life as a civilized society has become such that it can in the end not remain divided between opposing groups. The impact of war on the life of every man, woman and child, the havoc wrought, the exertion required, have become deeply resented by the nations.

But even apart from its military effects the interdependence of the world is clear. Western Germany cannot live without East Germany, but neither can industrialized Western Europe live without the agricultural East; nor can Asia raise its standards of living without the technical aid from the West, nor can North

America subsist without the commodities of the southern part of that continent, nor can any civilized part of the world maintain its way of living without access to the immense industrial production of the United States.

Under these circumstances the desire for world peace and for some form of world order is no longer a pious ideal, but a stark necessity of self-preservation. The one world is not here yet, but sooner or later it is inevitable.

A united world will not come about through the implementation of some neatly devised scheme, charter or constitution. It is being shaped through the bare logic of events, as a result of hard political and economic necessities. And it must come either by peaceful or by forceful means.

Theoretically one might conceive of a third possibility. The cold war between the communist and democratic worlds might continue indefinitely, punctuated by armed "border clashes" such as in Korea and Indo-China, in the same way as the Christian and the Moslem worlds faced and fought each other for centuries without the one ever definitely conquering or absorbing the other.

Is this possibility likely to materialize?

No one can predict how long the present state of tension will last. But to this author it seems unlikely that it could become a semi-permanent state like that which once existed between Christians and Moslems or between Babylonia and Assyria. The present situation differs from those in the two fundamental respects already mentioned: the scope of total warfare and the interdependence of the modern world as a result of technological development.

The first implies that, contrary to situations of the past where the normal life of a nation could more or less continue while wars were being fought at its frontiers, armed clashes between the two antagonistic groups of today would sooner or later touch off the total war for which they are prepared.

The second difference implies that if armed clashes were absent for a sufficient time to inaugurate a really peaceful co-existence, the process of interaction and mutual influence would inevitably bring about a certain degree of amalgamation. In the long run, therefore, it seems more likely that the present state of cold war will not endure without end; it will find a solution either the peaceful way or the forceful way.

XIII

The Peaceful Way: The Blend of East and West

A S THE phalanxes of the opposing millions are being drawn up for battle there is yet time for an appeal to reason.

There is no sensible reason on earth why a peaceful coexistence side by side of the democratic and communist worlds should not be possible, why each could not be perfectly happy and prosper in its own area without bothering the other—if only the Marxist-Leninist dogma of the world revolution of the proletariat did not prevent this blissful situation.

The existence of the Soviet Republic side by side with imperialist states for a long time is unthinkable. One or the other must triumph in the end, and before that end comes, a series of frightful clashes between the Soviet Republic and the bourgeois-states will be inevitable.

Lenin wrote these words in 1919 in the Report of the Central Committee at the eighth Party Congress. Somewhat later Stalin laid it down that the greatest problem of the Russian Revolution is "the need to promote the world revolution." And the same fundamental theme is summarized in this title of a section of the program of the Communist International: "The ultimate aim of the Communist International: World Communism." As long as this credo stands, it will constitute an insurmountable obstacle to the peaceful coexistence of the two political systems.

There are no signs that the leaders of world communism intend to drop this credo otherwise than as a temporary stratagem. Yet, if we are to stand with a clear conscience before the judgment of history, we must forever remain open to such a possibility, should it really offer itself. Internal changes of a political or economic or personal nature may shape up in Russia or China, which could for a considerable time eliminate the threat of communism to the external world: economic crises, internal strife, palace revolutions, struggle for the succession to leadership are occurrences by no means unknown in the history of autocratic states. On its part the free world is now in the process of building a degree of strength which may for a prolonged period make aggressive undertakings seem very inadvisable to the communist leaders.

If any of these contingencies should occur the free world will certainly not put up any obstacles to a peaceful coexistence, as the words and deeds of Western statesmen have borne out over and over again.

If a period of real peace and greater freedom of intercourse should be brought about, this would inevitably mean that the two worlds would start to influence each other's life and conceptions. Incompatible as the democratic and Marxist forms of society may be in the extreme forms propagated in the United States and Russia respectively, the best elements of each would nevertheless not fail to influence the other, narrowing the gap between them to a point where they need not constantly face each other with daggers drawn.

Many countries in Europe have successfully blended elements of the democratic and Marxist ideologies. Denmark, Sweden and

Norway have all three for a long period been ruled by governments which applied elements of Marxist socialism combined with those of economic and individual freedom, yet they have over decades maintained a high standard of living, a fairly stable prosperity and a relatively even spread of well-being over their classes. Belgium has under a similar system achieved one of the most spectacular postwar comebacks of Europe. The Netherlands, under a succession of governments which combined representatives of socialist, Christian and free-enterprise philosophies, made its economic recovery without one major strike occurring since the war's end, an unparalleled feat of labor-management relations. Critics, both inside and outside those countries, may hold that better results could have been achieved through the unadulterated application of a different economic and political system, either one way or the other, but the correctness of that contention is not under discussion here. The point at issue is whether a blend is possible and whether it can work; both questions have by the above and other experiences been answered in the affirmative.

Even the two main protagonists of the opposing system have in practice not been able to apply their theories without mixing in ingredients of the opposite system, no matter how reluctantly or how unconsciously.

In politics the democracies, though maintaining the essential principle that all power is derived from the people through parliament, have for decades shown a development toward an ever-increasing power of the central administration.

In economics, though a varying degree of free competition is maintained in nearly all democracies, it is hedged in by a nationally established framework, which, for instance in time of war, may closely approach that of the totalitarian state. Even in America the element of guided economy has never quite disappeared since the New Deal.

In the commerce and industry of the democracies private enterprise and private ownership are still the rule rather than the exception. Yet, as James Burnham has pointed out in *The Managerial Revolution*, the real control even in private enterprise has shifted from the stockholders toward the managers. One can realistically admit this trend without jumping to the conclusion that in the end all power and means of production must necessarily become concentrated in the state. The trend has been, and still is, toward a shift in power to the governments, the managers, the executives, the labor leaders. But the fundamental difference from a society run on the "Führer principle" remains that their power is not *imposed upon*, but *derived from* the people, the voters, the stockholders, the laborers.

In their social structure, furthermore, the democracies have for decades shown a constant narrowing of the differences between classes as a result of constantly rising taxes in the higher income brackets and of expanding social legislation. They have thus grown closer to the social equality which was originally a Marxist ideal.

On its side communist society has shown a more striking opposite tendency: to reinstate certain elements formerly held characteristic of the capitalist system or of bourgeois society. Lenin once said that bureaucracy and a standing army were characteristic of the bourgeois state; today Soviet Russia has the largest bureaucracy and the largest army in the world. Since the New Economic Policy of 1921 the Soviet Union has been obliged to reintroduce certain elements of the free-enterprise economy. For although the private business and private farming allowed by the N.E.P. were later abolished, an increasing inequality of compensation has been introduced into its economy in the form of diversified remuneration, incentive bonuses, priorities, privileges, etc. It has also reverted to such bourgeois values as strong family ties, large numbers of children, prevention of abortion (originally encouraged in the Soviet Union), tolerance of religion, income tax, reintroduction of protocol, uniforms and etiquette. A distinguished diplomat, Sir David Kelly, returning from Moscow in 1951 after a two-year tour of duty there, reported in the *New York Times Magazine* on the "counter-revolution in Russia":

> The early revolutionaries held all the traditional ideas associated with Western socialism—on internationalism, patriotism, marriage, the family, education, religion, the supremacy of the proletariat and a general vague sympathy with modernity for its own sake in literature and art. The new Soviet State is being built on the negation of the traditional Socialist attitude on every one of these points. This process—the main outlines of which are becoming visible—may fairly be called the counter-revolution. . . .
>
> In all matters relating to morals and the family Russia has become definitely reactionary and far the most puritanical country known to me. . . .
>
> The most unexpected and radical transformation has been the complete abandonment in practice of the proletarian society with its inseparable ideal of social equality. . . . They are moving away from social equality as fast as the West is trying to approach it.

It is highly probable that if the iron curtain were raised, if only a few inches, the breeze of fresh air entering would stir all life behind it. In the ensuing battle of ideas the outcome would depend upon the vigor of the ideas of both sides, once they were liberated from the fetters of propaganda and from the influence of armed force.

The West has no reason to fear such a struggle-without-arms and every reason to welcome it. Where it should prove too weak to win, it would only deserve to be beaten by new and stronger concepts.

If, however, the West is still healthy and strong, it has nothing to fear from such a contest. In the material field it can offer higher living standards through technical progress; in the spiritual encounter with communism Western civilization has still these imperishable propositions to offer:

That man is not made for the state but the state for man.

That the people were not made to serve their rulers, but rulers to serve the people.

That man was created to serve the purpose of his Creator, not the Creator to serve the purpose of the state.

It is not the West which has in the past evaded a contest of ideas. It will not be the West which evades it in the future. The peaceful way is still open.

XIV

The Forceful Way: If War Comes

WHY THE WEST WOULD WIN

THE peaceful road to a harmonious coexistence, then, is still open. The choice between war and peace lies with the Kremlin. We, on our part, can offer reasonable terms of co-operation and can try to bring about a situation of strength likely to deter aggression, but the ultimate decision lies not in our hands. Such is the fate of the peaceful.

Unfortunately a long succession of events has shown that communism is bent on extending its rule over ever new areas whenever it thinks that this can be done without retaliation. It is not sufficiently realized that in the ten years from 1939 to 1949 communism expanded its area of control from 170 million to 770 million people.

It is therefore necessary reluctantly to take into consideration the possibility that the amalgamation of the two worlds may, as often before in history, come about through a clash of arms.

If this armed conflict should occur it would in all probability be the final battle of Western civilization. Its role would be analogous to that of the war between Mark Antony and Octavianus in the classic civilization, which brought the whole area then covered by that civilization under one leadership: the universal state was established.

But the modern counterpart of this struggle would be on a scale a thousand times larger and more destructive. It is no exaggeration to say that this would be the greatest and fiercest clash which has yet occurred in the history of mankind, fought with the most destructive weapons ever produced. When Xerxes set out for the conquest of Greece he probably had an army of some 10,000 under his command. Alexander the Great marched into Asia at the head of 30,000 men. When Napoleon started his Russian campaign he had assembled the largest army then known in history, numbering 500,000 men.

All this is a mere trifle compared to the masses that will be thrown into battle if World War III ever breaks out. Well over ten million men and women will stand in uniform on both sides, hundreds of millions of civilians behind them will slave on the tasks assigned to them, suffering hardly less hardship, running hardly smaller risks. Cities and whole countries will be ravaged and ruined; the hollow-eyed skeletons of Warsaw, Coventry and Berlin will be multiplied. Yet, there is something worse: submission to tyranny—a word with very real sense to the millions who have lived under it.

Therefore war, with all its horror is a *risk* that must be taken if it becomes absolutely sure that it is the only way to prevent the *certainty* of the destruction of Western civilization by communism. The material damage to be expected is always less serious than the complete subversion of the human mind inherent in surrender to a totalitarian system. Men fighting for freedom have always, when the choice was inevitable, chosen to risk annihilation rather than surrender. Whenever a nation or a civilization chose the other alternative it was doomed.

But the choice must indeed be inevitable. If ever the West takes up arms, we must be certain that we have neglected nothing to prevent it, and have done nothing to bring it about.

Also we must, as responsible and realistic men, weigh the outcome. If war is forced upon it, can the West win?

It will. There can be no doubt about the outcome: in a full-scale armed conflict the West would win in the end.

There are four principal reasons why it would. Two are of a material, two of a spiritual nature.

Industrial Potential

First of all the West possesses the greatest industrial potential. World War III, if it comes, will be a battle of production as much as the last war, and a battle of technology and science even more than the last. In both industrial war potential and technological progress the West is well ahead of the communist world, even though the monopoly of the atomic bomb is gone.

A few figures will illustrate its productive superiority. (The production figures for the Soviet Union are based on the statistics contained in Mr. Malenkov's report to the nineteenth Communist Party Congress in October, 1952, but they are fairly well confirmed by estimates of the United Nations Economic Commission for Europe and other Western experts.)

The total *crude steel* production of Russia and its European satellites in 1952 was estimated at 51 million net tons, against 113 million tons (capacity) in the U.S.A. and 70 million tons in free Europe. For 1953 the United Nations estimates are: 55 million tons for Russia and satellites, 118 million for the U.S.A., and 72 millions for free Europe.

Coal output of Russia and its satellites in 1952 was estimated at over 300 million tons, against 551 million tons in the U.S.A. and 472 million tons in Western Europe.

Electricity production in the U.S.S.R. and its satellites for 1952 was estimated at 117 billion kilowatt hours, against ±400 billion in the U.S.A. and well over half that amount in Western Europe.

Oil production in Russia and its satellites in 1952 was estimated at 1,060,000 barrels per day, or 8 per cent of world production, as against 6,700,000 barrels per day or 52 per cent of world production in the U.S.A. (for the whole of the Western hemisphere even over 70 per cent), and 2,250,000 barrels or 16 per cent in the Middle East.

In order to put these figures in the correct perspective and not draw overoptimistic conclusions from them, several things must be kept in mind.

The first is that in the communist-ruled countries a far smaller share of the available total of basic raw materials goes into civilian consumption than in the democratic countries. Hence a comparison of industrial productive strength based merely on the total production figures is apt to lead to overoptimistic conclusions.

In addition it seems, according to experts who have studied these matters closely, that average Soviet output of arms per unit of raw materials used is higher than in the U.S.A.

In the third place it is insufficiently realized that the Soviet output of raw materials has for the last decade been growing at a surprising rate, *which in some important categories is percentagewise even higher than in the U.S.A. or Western Europe.* Thus Russian steel production in 1952 had increased by nearly 90 per cent over 1940, coal production by 80 per cent and electricity output by 140 per cent over 1940.

Finally it must be realized that the Soviet Union is well on its way to achieve or even surpass the targets proclaimed by Premier Stalin in his speech in the Bolshoi Theater in February, 1946, as necessary for Russia's safety, which probably meant: necessary in order to be able to carry on a long war. The first column below gives the figures he then said had to be achieved around 1960 or 1965, and which seemed preposterous when compared to the then last available production figures, those for 1940. These are mentioned in the second column, whereas the third column gives the actual production for 1952 and the fourth the targets of the Fifth Five Year Plan for 1955, which on the basis of the 1952 production and the rate of increase of the last few years seem likely to be attained. All are exclusive of production in the satellite countries.

	Original target for 1960-65	*1940 production*	*1952 production*	*Revised 1955 target*
		(in millions of metric tons)		
Pig iron	50	15	25	34
Crude steel	60	18.3	35	44.7
Coal	500	166	300	377
Oil	60	31	47	69.5

In order to realize how close the 1955 targets are bringing the Soviet bloc as a whole to the minimum safety requirements originally intended to be fulfilled by 1960 or 1965, the former must be augmented by the production figures of the satellite countries, which are difficult to ascertain, but in some categories are substantial.

The 1953 steel output of these countries, for instance, is estimated at 13 million tons. Assuming that this amount will by 1955 have risen to about 16 million tons, it follows that by that year the total domestic and satellite production available to the Soviet area will have reached a quantity which was scheduled to be reached only by 1960 or 1965.

Also it can be seen that the new 1955 target for oil for the Soviet Union alone, not counting satellite production, is already well above the original 1960-65 target. Thus it must be assumed that *for some important raw materials the minimum "safety" targets proclaimed by Stalin in 1946 may be reached five to ten years ahead of the scheduled time.* Since industrial potential is nowadays the primary factor in determining a country's capacity to sustain war, and consequently its capacity to follow a foreign policy that implies the risk of war, the ominous significance of the above figures can hardly be overestimated.

Yet, even taking these factors into account, the figures mentioned show clearly that the resources at the disposal of communism are still well inferior to those of the free world; on the other hand it is clear that they would nearly equal or even outstrip those of the Western hemisphere if Western Europe, the Middle East and Southeast Asia were to come under its sway. If that were allowed to happen, the Eurasian continent would become a virtually unassailable fortress and the odds, even in a long-range war, would be heavily against the Western Hemisphere. The situation then prevailing was described by President Eisenhower in his last report as Army Chief of Staff in 1948 in the following words:

> America's security would be in dire danger. We would find ourselves facing across narrowing ocean and Arctic barriers a despotic colossus spread over and beyond the combined Eurasian territories of the Roman Empire, the Persia of antiquity, the Germanic Kings and the Mongol Khans.

Sea and Air Power

A second element which, next to productive superiority, is likely to warrant victory of the West is its naval superiority, which in a war of long duration would sooner or later be matched by its air superiority.

More than half a century has elapsed since Admiral Mahan wrote his classic on *The Influence of Sea Power upon History*. Today the relative value of the navy, army and air force in modern warfare is a hotly debated issue. That discussion is often clouded by interservice rivalry, thus confusing the question of the contribution which each service made to the victory in a particular war or campaign with the fundamental thesis of

Mahan. The latter never pretended that the navy was superior to the army in the sense that the one could defeat the other or that wars could be won with a navy alone. What he did prove was that throughout history nations which possessed superiority at sea in the end usually win out over others, even though the latter may possess strong armies. The reason for this is not that a navy can defeat an army, but that an army, however victorious it may be, finds its natural limitation at the seashore, which it cannot overcome but for the possession of superiority at sea. An opponent possessing that superiority, on the other hand, can withdraw in safety behind the water and bide his time until he has built an army of superior strength, in the meantime harassing the continental power constantly along his coast and cutting off his overseas supplies in men and material, of which the army in the long run is bound to run short. The continental power is therefore pressed for time, whereas the naval power has time on its side and can wait to choose the moment when and the place where its army is likely to be superior; for the final victory has always got to be won by the army.

Does this time-honored axiom still hold true in the era of air and atomic warfare?

As regards the first part of the question, it seems unnecessary with a view to a possible third World War, to consider whether a naval power could hold out against an enemy possessing combined superiority both in the air and on the land, since it is unlikely that the West would suffer from a serious inferiority in the air other than perhaps initially and temporarily. The situation as it is likely to present itself in a third World War is that one side would start off with overwhelming superiority on land, the other with a similar superiority on the seas, with neither overwhelmingly superior in the air.

Without going into a detailed analysis of the experience of World War II it must be pointed out that none of the victories constituting the *main turning points* of that war (as distinct from final victories), such as the Battle of Britain, the Battle of the Atlantic, El Alamein, the invasion of North Africa, the invasion of Europe, Pearl Harbor, the Battles of the Coral Sea and of Midway, could have been won without superiority at sea or without sufficient air strength to prevent the enemy from dominating the skies. It shows that even in the last war, notwithstanding the tremendous role played by the air force, neither the latter nor the army in themselves could turn the tide: the turning points depended upon the control of the seas, given sufficient air coverage.

If World War III ever comes, it is bound to be the most gigantic and grim test that has ever taken place or can be imagined of the decisive importance of naval power. For whereas the air forces on both sides are likely to be more or less equal, at least after the initial stage and when taken *in toto* (with a communist advantage in fighters and a Western advantage in bombers), it is obvious that in that same stage there is bound to be a considerable numerical superiority at sea in favor of the democratic navies, notwithstanding the tremendous challenge of the Soviet submarine fleet.

The second point which remains doubtful is whether the influence of sea power is eliminated by the application of atomic weapons.

This question, too, can only receive a final answer in actual warfare; the last war produced no experience of the effect of atomic weapons against warships. For the moment one can only say that the trial tests at Eniwetok seem to indicate that atomic bombs will not eliminate the value of a navy.

A third question arises, to which it is less difficult to figure out an answer: Is the influence of sea power eliminated by the continent-wide size of the area controlled by a continental opponent?

Hitler at the moment of the widest extension of his power controlled an almost self-contained triangular land mass stretching from the Pyrenees to the White Sea and to the Caucasus, and for some time there was much talk in the Axis camp about holding out indefinitely in this fortress Europe, and limiting warfare to the repulsion of enemy attacks on it. That system did not work.

If World War III should embrace the present area of both opposing camps, the land mass controlled by communism would be larger than has ever been the case in history. Even if communism should not succeed in further extending its present dominium, it would cover a territory from the Elbe to the Pacific and from the Antarctic to the Himalayas, containing 770 million inhabitants.

The figures for the output of some essential commodities mentioned earlier in this chapter, however, show that even this vast area would be seriously defective in war potential on particular sectors as long as it does not possess (a) the industrial potential, the know-how and the skilled labor of Western Europe, (b) the oil of the Middle East, and (c) the tin and rubber of Southeast Asia. It is therefore a vital necessity for communism to bring these three regions under its sway, and as vital a necessity for the democracies to prevent this. If these three key areas were to fall into communist hands, then there seems to be no reason why the communist world could not, as far as its *resources* are concerned, hold out indefinitely. In that respect the effect of naval superiority upon a continental power of that size might indeed become negligible. It retains, however, even against such a colossus, its *military* advantage in that the continental power cannot invade the enemy over a sea it does not control, or through an air space it does not dominate, whereas the naval power can choose its moment and place for invasion. This latter aspect of the domination of the seas would in a future war probably still be as valid as it was on D-day, 1944, when military air transportation had already taken on very sizable proportions.

In conclusion it can be said that in the gigantic struggle of

naval against land power the former would, if backed by adequate air power, retain *most* of its traditional decisive influence
as long as the continental power were limited to the present communist territory, and would retain *part* of its influence even if
that territory were extended to include some of the key areas it
now lacks.

But wars are not won by material and military force alone,
indispensable as these are. In the end wars are won by the
vigor and the perseverance of the combatants, and these depend
upon their conviction of fighting for a cause worth the sacrifices
it requires. All great wars sooner or later reach a stage of military
equilibrium; it is then that the mental and spiritual factors start
to dominate the outcome. They cannot by themselves defeat guns
and tanks; but when guns and tanks get deadlocked it is the
spirit which tips the scales. It cannot be subdued by brute force.
The body can be torn asunder by gunfire and crushed by tanks;
but the spirit escapes unconquered to inspire hundreds who
follow. In the end the spirit always wins out.

It is this fundamental truth which is invariably overlooked by
the dictators of all times; it is the spirit for which their secret
police hunt, because it escapes their orders, their concentration
camps, their incinerators.

As long as there is one soul alive who refuses to submit to the
almighty power of Party and State, the creative spirit is not
extinguished and will one day rise again to inspire men to revolt
against tyranny.

In the struggle with communism the democracies have on their
side two forces to which the spirit has always rallied and on
which dictatorships have invariably shattered: freedom and
religion.

Freedom

Ever since the birth of mankind man has craved freedom—the
right to live, to think, to worship according to his convictions;

he has been endowed by his Creator with the unalienable right to life, liberty and the pursuit of happiness.

In our time this age-old ideal has taken on a new meaning. It means freedom from certain blessings of the totalitarian regime: the knock on the door in the night, the departure from which there is no return; the spying of sons on fathers, of wives on husbands; the fear of uttering a word that will provoke the wrath of the Party; the concentration camp, summit of scientifically applied cruelty.

These notions have scant significance for those who have up to now had the privilege of escaping life under a totalitarian regime. All the more bitter is their significance for those who have not been so fortunate. To them the daily prayer "God, make us free" is more essential than "Give us our daily bread." It is the inner tragedy of freedom that the call for freedom will always rally to its banner those craving it, but they disband once victory is achieved and the goal seems reached. We, to whom freedom has become as common as the water from the faucet, must bring ourselves to realize that freedom is a treasure requiring eternal vigilance; and above all that freedom is more severely threatened today than ever it was, because the present threat comes from an ideology which has the globe itself as its target. If it wins there will be no escaping it; it will accompany you on the road, it will follow you into the woods where you will try to flee it, it will be with you in your bedroom, it will demand your *total* allegiance, every ounce of your energy, your thought, your heart. If we realize this danger and make it abundantly plain to the world, liberty will be our strongest ally, an undefeatable ally as old as the world.

One of the reasons why the Greeks won out over the numerically superior Persians was, says Herodotus, that they felt that the subjects of a despot are no match for the citizens of a free state, for these yield obedience only to a law which is self-imposed.

Religion

Allied with us, too, in the case of a new World War would be religion.

The totalitarian state, which cannot tolerate any allegiance but to itself, is the mortal enemy of religion. It can never, at the price of abdication, acknowledge that the soul owes its ultimate allegiance outside this world. Therefore in the struggle between the free world and communism all religious creeds can not but in the end line up against this pseudo-church which is trying to take their place—and this applies to Protestant and Catholic, to Moslem and Hindu alike. But to us who belong to Western civilization the commandment issued two thousand years ago to love our neighbor is still a better way to a just world than the commandment issued one hundred years ago to hate and destroy certain groups of society.

It is disturbing that the Christian basis of our civilization is in some countries much less frequently mentioned than democracy as one of the main pillars of our ideology. Yet it is even more fundamental and goes deeper than the latter. The Christian faith is at the root of our democracy, not the other way around. If we abandon that foundation our civilization will be like a tooth of which the nerve has been killed: outwardly it will look the same and stand for some time, but its disintegration will only be a matter of time. And without this spiritual background Western civilization will never be able to assert itself to the masses inside or outside its realm, to whom the soul means more than even democracy or prosperity.

XV

America's Destiny

THE readings of history are clear: Western civilization is about to enter a new phase, the epoch of one civilization-wide world and civilization-wide peace. In all civilizations this is the last phase; it can also be the greatest, if greatness is measured in the greatest good for the greatest number. It can be an era like the Principate in Rome or the Middle and New Empire in Egypt. Its value to contemporary man and history, as well as its duration, will depend upon its inner strength and creative force.

In this one world, whether it comes about through peace or through war, the United States of America is by history destined to play a preponderant part. It is only fair to say that it has not desired this part which has been thrust upon it by force of circumstances. It must also be said that once America realized that it had been forced into the position of the involuntary protagonist, it was remarkably quick to adapt to it. Earlier in this book it has been pointed out that, notwithstanding criticism and mistakes, U.S. foreign policy after World War II has shown courage, vision, and a generosity toward others unknown in history. The creative force apparent in these qualities opens up boundless possibilities.

On the other hand there are many pitfalls ahead. Nothing is easier for a power in the unthankful role of world leader than to stumble into these by overlooking some fundamental conditions it is expected to fulfill.

REQUIREMENTS OF LEADERSHIP

It should never be forgotten that all leadership, and particularly democratic leadership, derives its authority from the consent of those it leads. No leadership in history, whether of dictator, monarch, class or state, has ever endured when it failed to hold the inner assent of its followers. Toynbee's conception of a creative minority guiding a responsive majority applies to the community of states as well as to that of citizens.

The other countries of the democratic world are sufficiently realistic to recognize that the United States, which contributes more political, military and economic power than any other nation, is for that reason destined to be their leader. What they fear, however, and what they would strongly resent and resist is to be ruled instead of guided—dictation instead of co-operation. They recognize the United States as *primus inter pares*, but they have not so bitterly fought dictators of other countries in order to submit to dictation within their own community. The great question is whether United States leadership will be voluntarily followed from inner conviction or resentfully from bare necessity. The answer will depend upon the extent to which America will be able to avoid certain mistakes upon which former world powers have foundered and thus make its leadership acceptable.

Spiritual Leadership

This is the first and foremost requirement. The world has too strongly the impression that American leadership limits itself to grants of material aid and attempts to improve living conditions.

Far be it from us to underestimate the importance of either of these two factors. The Marshall Plan aid to Europe, for instance, has been an indispensable help in restoring that continent's economy after the war. To raise the living standards of the millions who still exist in the basest poverty and squalor is, as has been pointed out before, one of the three main challenges to

Western civilization. Only by providing food to eat and a place to sleep to these masses can their sense of being underprivileged be overcome and the value which our economic system has for them be proven.

But neither of these steps will suffice to win over a nation. No nation, as no man, will accept another's guidance merely because the other is wealthier and prepared to share some of his wealth with him. On the contrary, the sad truth is that between nations, as between men, this seems to make for resentment rather than for gratitude.

Men will be attracted, but will never be inspired, by the prospect of more bathrooms or refrigerators. The battle for the minds of the millions will not be won by holding out to them better plumbing or faster cars, particularly in continents like Europe and Asia where the spirit has always reigned supreme. And this applies especially in competition with an opponent who has succeeded in combining in his propaganda a rosy picture of a classless society with an ideology replacing the altars of religion. Against this pseudo-religion the West can only win out if it has something more to offer than food and television.

As such it possesses two spiritual values which are at its basis and have not been surpassed yet: religion and democracy. In the American picture presented to the world the latter is far more conspicuous than the former; yet the former is as essential as the latter, not only to Western civilization, but to any individual it wants to convince. The human soul is not satisfied to stop at what the eye perceives: "The eye is not satisfied with seeing, nor the ear filled with hearing." That applies in Kiev as in Santiago or in Timbuktu. Only by the force of its spiritual faith and of its democratic ideology can the West meet the present supreme challenge to its existence.

Respect for the Independence of Others

"Sovereignty," no matter how often it may still be used as a catchword, is in its original significance virtually extinguished in our present world as a result of ever-increasing interdependence. Few countries, including the United States and Russia, can today afford to make decisions completely without regard to others.

At the same time it is essential that in the coming one world all nations should not be submerged in one amalgamated uniform mass. Politically it would be disastrous if all power were centered in one place without a counterweight to balance it. Economically, too, it can be a lopsided and unwholesome situation, as we have seen after World War II, if large areas are unable to maintain a balanced economy and have to depend on outside aid. Spiritually it would mean the ossification of Western civilization if the many contributing sources from which it has sprung were to dry up and be replaced by one tap with chlorinated water. Diversity has been the mainspring of our culture; uniformity would be its end.

It may be useful to revert here to one of the laws which Danilevsky wrote down nearly a century ago:

A civilization . . . reaches its fullness, variety and richness only when its "ethnographic material" is diverse and when these ethnographic elements are not swallowed by one body politic, but enjoy independence and make up a federation or political system of states.

And applying this test to practice he states that the richest and fullest civilizations so far have been the Greek and the European, because of the variety of their "ethnographic material" and of the autonomy of the several political units that have been the builders and bearers of these civilizations.

The role of leader among nations, as among men, is a hard and thankless one; criticism is due to be sharp, abundant and unreasonable, appreciation meager and inconspicuous; satisfaction can only be derived from the sense of fulfilling a historic duty; fair judgment can only be expected beyond our time or beyond our world.

But the ingratitude and lack of appreciation which are bound to befall a leader should never induce him to ignore all criticism and impose his will. True leadership rests on persuasion, not on coercion. Some of the greatest leading nations in history, such as the Romans or the British, who for centuries kept together an empire of heterogeneous elements, knew the value of this wisdom. Often they applied cunning and force, sometimes ruthlessly, but in the end they could only rule as long as they commanded the consent of the ruled. This requires tremendous, almost superhuman, self-restraint. The inclination is strong for anyone who knows that ultimately he will have to bear the consequences to impose his own will; the man who foots the bill will want to decide about the expenses. Yet, even so, he will in a partnership be wise to exercise the utmost care always to act in consultation with his partners, respect their personalities and above all: *not try to model them after his own image.*

True leadership brings about what Toynbee calls *mimesis,* voluntary imitation on the part of the followers. Mimesis of America can be seen in a thousand small aspects of present-day life all over the globe: in the Paris newsstands the French magazines are almost crowded out by *Life, Time* and *Look*; cocktails are served from Singapore to Lisbon; American cigarettes, once disliked abroad for their strong taste, are now the smartest thing to offer from Capetown to North Cape; Hollywood reigns supreme in cinemas all over the world; even in the most "anti-imperialist" of Asian nations one finds that the most coveted mark of success is the possession of a Cadillac; and the first thing which met this author upon landing in Bangkok in search for the artistic beauties of Siam was an enormous truck full of Coca-Cola.

As long as this peaceful penetration of American habits results from a natural process of osmosis, it is inevitable and unobjectionable from a point of view of effective leadership, even though the loss of national and local characteristics may be highly regrettable from a cultural point of view. The danger to the leadership comes where the "guiding minority" tries to *impose* its views or its habits. This would happen, for instance, if America should try to introduce everywhere the exact form of economy applied in America, or if it should try to abolish all monarchies as anachronisms.

Such imposition in disregard of national traditions not only renders a civilization poorer and therefore weaker, but at the same time evokes resentment against the leadership. Respect of the rights and peculiarities of the minority by the majority, like those of the governed by the rulers, is the essence of democracy.

It took the political genius of Alexander the Great to establish a sound balance between his imperial supersystem and the autonomy of the Greek *polis*. It will be the almost superhuman task and test of American statesmanship in a modern world to strike the right balance between the guidance of others and the respect of their independence.

The Living Example

There are many other pitfalls, of course, which the experience of previous civilizations points out.

Corruption is one of the illnesses which has in the last phase of a society often undermined the prestige and—more serious—the moral fiber of the leading nation.

Wealth, too abundantly enjoyed by few, or too long sustained by many, is a comfortable mattress on which many a world power has gone to sleep. This is an unpopular thing to say in a world where the pursuit of prosperity almost seems to have become the very purpose of life; yet it is necessary to say it, because the road of history is littered with the skeletons of civilizations that did not wake up in time; they died of opulence, not of want.

Personal rivalries between tycoons, taking the place of the former national wars, in which men were prepared to die for their ideals or their country, are equally characteristic of the closing phase of each civilization. The greatness and duration of that period depend largely on the extent to which the fundamental bases of the civilization are kept alive and personal strife kept subservient to the struggle of ideas which is the characteristic of every living civilization.

The Danger of Political Hegemony

The continued and uncontested exercise of economic or political power without competition or the possibility of change, is bound to corrode the force exercising it. "Power corrupts, and absolute power corrupts absolutely." This applies in a community of nations as well as within one state. Therefore it would be fatal both to the United States and to Western civilization if the United States should have an absolute monopoly of power. Monopolistic power is bound to get to assert itself for its own sake and for that of its bearers, rather than for the sake of the community, as the history of all dictatorships shows. That is why we have for decades now been fighting one-party regimes. That is why the U.S. Congress restricts economic monopolies.

In the Western one world competition could no longer take the form of military conflicts. But that does not mean there should not be a certain rivalry and balance of forces both within and without it. India, China, Russia, Latin America will all be centers of economic and political gravity. But within the Western world the natural area of counterbalance is Europe. Before we discuss the part which Europe must play as counterweight to America it is necessary to stress another vital basis for American stewardship:

Maintenance of the Common Heritage with Europe

Europe is the source of Western civilization, not only in the sense that it originated in medieval Italy and France, not only in the sense that North and South America were populated from Europe. In Europe Western Civilization still has many of its spiritual roots; it is there that much of its creative force is still operative, as we found when analyzing that force in Part II of this book. Impressive and vigorous as the economic and political forces are that have come to life on the American soil it would be an irreparable loss if it were to be cut off from its European roots, if the benefits were to be lost that accrue from this inter-action between two worlds.

America might survive for some time as a glamorous and powerful state, but it would, like similar states in previous civiliza-tions, never overcome the separation from its roots. It would be-come a magnificent but petrified society, a moonlight civilization, swirling through the spaces of history like a brilliant phenomenon, a meteor burning itself out because it was torn away from the fire that generated it.

XVI

Europe's Part

IT IS time, too, to take stock of Europe's assets—not in pos-sessions, which are a product of the past, but in creative po-tential, which will determine its future—and to decide upon the role it can play in the developing unity of the Western world.

From the array of creative forces enumerated in Chapter X it can be concluded that in the cultural field Europe is, far from being exhausted, still actively productive. The architecture, the music, the films, the books, it has produced in the last decades are proof of its creative vitality in the artistic field. It seems a safe assumption that unless Western Europe should again become a battlefield and be destroyed beyond recuperation, it will continue for a considerable time to be a main source of Western civilization in the cultural field, even if its political and economic importance should further decline. In the same way after Alexander the Great the cultural influence of Greece pervaded both the Eastern and the Western parts of the ancient world. Thanks to the political achievement of Alexander in welding his extended realm into one cultural unity with a common language, art and political organization, Greek influence permeated that whole area and in the East Roman Empire even survived the fall of Rome for a millennium. Yet the Great Age of Greece was irretrievably gone; its culture was disseminated over the civilized world, but the roots of the plant itself had died.

Is Europe to content itself with that role?

There is no reason why it should. The economic and political forces which have enabled it for centuries now to stride in the vanguard of nations are still there.

Whether Europe will survive as a leading factor in the world depends on its capacity to adapt itself to the necessity of integration. A surprisingly strong crop of forces has sprung up all over Europe working toward that goal. They have already resulted in an intricate structure of organizations, from the Council of Europe to the European Defense Community. Endless hindrances are obstructing their success, but these creative forces are there, and vigorously alive. It now depends on the speed of their success whether the integration of free Europe will be achieved and its economic and military strength restored in time to save the continent from a new world conflict. It is a race against time, a race against the forces of aggression, and at the same time a race against the factors effecting its own degradation. If free Europe succeeds in winning that race, then, and only then, its 300 million people can become a fully equivalent and therefore more valuable partner of the United States in a balanced North Atlantic community. We are not thinking of a "third power," a neutral between two ideological camps; Europe will

always stand for the principles of Christianity, freedom and democracy which have ever constituted the lifeblood of its civilization, well before America existed.

But if Europe is not to become a colony of the United States
it must determine its own policy, its own constitutional and economic structure, its own way of life. This can only be achieved if
Europe is sufficiently integrated politically to follow a common
over-all policy, and economically to render mass production and
consumption possible and make the continent independent of
outside aid. It is a proof of great wisdom that the United States
has with regard to Europe never followed the Roman device of
"divide et impera," but urged for its unification.

There is no danger of armed conflict between a united Europe
and the United States; their interdependence of interests and community of ideals would prevent it. But as we pointed out before
it is essential for healthy leadership in any community that there
be a counterweight to it, able to offer criticism and competition,
ready to take over if necessary. To achieve that aim it will also
be necessary for Europe to keep in mind some other requirements
that are in danger of being overlooked today.

THE CULTURAL SUPERIORITY COMPLEX OF EUROPE

Both for the sake of Europe's good relations with other parts
of the world and for the sake of its own vitality it is essential that
Europeans should shed their innate conviction that their "culture" is superior to that of, say, America or Asia. Nothing is so
repugnant to both Americans and Asians as the attitude usually
adopted—often unconsciously—by West Europeans toward
people of other areas of the world: that as a matter of course
European culture has more tradition, is more deeply rooted and
more refined than that of others. Nothing warrants the complacent
assumption that other areas are not just as capable of producing
equal cultural products, or are not in fact doing so. What re-

mains of the age-old civilizations of the East, impregnated by the forces of its newborn nationalism, as well as the rising cultural achievements of America creates a serious challenge to Europe even in the cultural field. Nothing in the history of nations and of civilizations has been as conducive to a certain death of its spiritual vigor as self-complacency; that attitude is not only a sign but also an origin of decadence, and we Europeans should do well to realize it.

EUROPE'S POOR-RELATIVE COMPLEX

To Europe's feeling of cultural superiority, which is of old standing, there has been added since World War II one of incapacity to pay its own way and of dependence on outside help. There is even a certain connection between the two in that the sense of lost economic leadership has induced many Europeans to seek compensation in an inflated sense of their own cultural value. In such a situation it is a natural human inclination to make the excuse: If only I had met the same favorable circumstances I could have done even better. However, the only real salvation for old nations is to adapt their values to new circumstances and see to it that they again do better than others, as their forefathers did.

Nothing is as killing to initiative as the habit of reverting to others for economic or financial assistance. In times of transition such assistance may be necessary and beneficent as a stop-gap. But when prolonged beyond the period of absolute necessity it becomes a source of weakness. The threatening habit in many non-communist countries of expecting the United States to pay the deficit if the national economy runs in the red is as killing to their economic vigor as it is repellent to their self-esteem and repugnant to the United States. The sooner Europe becomes self-supporting and of its own initiative puts an end to foreign aid the better.

THE TREASURE OF EUROPEAN DIVERSITY

The need for European mass production and mass consumption, for a common defense, and for a common over-all policy should never put an end to the diversity which has always constituted one of the riches of European civilization. From the abbeys of Italy, France and Spain, from the cities of the Renaissance, from the Hansa towns in Germany and the Low Countries, from the Universities of Paris and Bologna, Prague and Heidelberg, Oxford and Louvain—from these sources all over Europe welled the waters that combined in the mainstream of European civilization. The political, economic and military integration of Europe will inevitably require the sacrifice of many local or national interests. But it should never aim at uniformity. The end of diversity would mean the end of Europe.

THE EUROPEAN HERITAGE OF CHRISTIANITY

It has been stated before that Western civilization had its cradle in the abbeys and cathedrals, in the sacred laws, the religious art and the monastic science of Medieval Europe. That Christian origin is as inseparable from European culture as its diversity or its sense of freedom. The Christian trend has always persisted strongly in Europe, even when humanism, with its offspring of rationalism and Marxism, rose as rival forces, and overshadowed it in America in the form of a predominantly secular society. No civilization has ever survived the death of its basic religion. That applies as much to Western civilization today as it has to others in the past. It is primarily up to Europe, where the Christian influence is still strongest, to uphold this heritage. It can not be better expressed than in these words of T. S. Eliot in his *Notes towards the Definition of Culture*:

> To our Christian heritage we owe many things besides religious faith. Through it we trace the evolution of our arts, through it we have our conception of Roman Law which has done so much to shape the Western

World, through it we have our conceptions of private and public morality. And through it we have our common standards of literature, in the literatures of Greece and Rome. The Western World has its unity in this heritage, in Christianity and in the ancient civilisations of Greece, Rome and Israel, from which, owing to two thousand years of Christianity, we trace our descent.

It is in Christianity that our arts have developed; it is in Christianity that the laws of Europe have—until recently—been rooted. It is against a background of Christianity that all our thought has significance. An individual European may not believe that the Christian faith is true, and yet what he says, and makes, and does, will all spring out of his heritage of Christian culture and depend upon that culture for its meaning. Only a Christian culture could have produced a Voltaire or a Nietzsche. I do not believe that the culture of Europe could survive the complete disappearance of the Christian Faith. And I am convinced of that not merely because I am a Christian myself, but as a student of social biology. If Christianity goes, the whole of our culture goes. Then you must start painfully again, and you cannot put on a new culture ready made. You must wait for the grass to grow to feed the sheep to give the wool out of which your new coat will be made. You must pass through many centuries of barbarism. We should not live to see the new culture, nor would our great-great-great-grandchildren: and if we did, not one of us would be happy in it.

If Europe can reinvigorate its fundamental values and by a supreme effort meet the challenges of this twentieth-century crisis there is no reason why it should not continue to be one of the leading forces in the world. Egypt came back after five centuries, Assyria after six centuries, Babylon after fifteen centuries; all had a New Empire, more splendid than the first. Each civilization can rise to yet greater heights, even in its so-called last phase, which we have not entered yet.

There is plenty of ground, as this book has attempted to prove, for faith that both Europe and America possess the creative force to conquer the present crisis of Western civilization and lead it to new peaks. The co-operation and the interaction of the old and the new worlds will, if they are both determined to do so, bring to further fruition that force which set in motion the brush of the

Medieval masters, inspired Beethoven's symphonies, motivated William the silent and George Washington, brought forth the Commonwealth of Nations, erected Notre Dame and Rockefeller Center: the creative spirit of the West.

It can be done. It depends on us.

BIBLIOGRAPHY

RAYMOND ARON, *Les Guerres en Chaine* (Paris, 1951).

HARRY ELMER BARNES, "Arnold Joseph Toynbee: Orosius and Augustine in Modern Dress," in *An Introduction to the History of Sociology*, pp. 717-736 (Chicago, 1948).

HARRY ELMER BARNES and HOWARD BECKER, *Contemporary Social History* (New York, 1940).

CHARLES AUSTIN BEARD, in *American Historical Review*, April, 1940.

HERBERT BUTTERFIELD, *Christianity and History* (New York, 1950).

ERWIN D. CANHAM, *Awakening, The World at Mid-Century* (New York, London, Toronto, 1951).

E. H. CARR, *The Soviet Impact on the Western World* (New York, 1947).

SHEPARD CLOUGH, *The Rise and Fall of Civilization* (New York, London, 1951).

R. G. COLLINGWOOD, in *The Idea of History* (New York 1946), pp. 159-165.

R. G. COLLINGWOOD, "Oswald Spengler and the Theory of Historical Cycles," in *Antiquity*, I, Sept., 1927, pp. 311-325.

EDWIN F. DAKIN, *Today and Destiny, Vital Excerpts from The Decline of the West of Oswald Spengler* (New York, 1940).

T. S. ELIOT, *Notes towards the Definition of Culture* (New York, 1949).

HERMAN FINER, *America's Destiny* (New York, 1947).

E. FISHER, *Passing of the European Age* (Cambridge, Mass., 1942).

P. GEYL and ARNOLD TOYNBEE, *Can We Know the Pattern of the Past?* Discussion broadcast by the B.B.C. (Bussum, 1948).

P. GEYL, P. SOROKIN and ARNOLD TOYNBEE, *The Pattern of the Past; Can We Determine It?* (Boston, 1949).

O. HANDLING, "Toynbee: In the Dark Backward," in *Partisan Review*, July-August, 1947.

GRANVILLE HICKS, "Arnold Toynbee: The Boldest Historian," in *Harper's Magazine*, February, 1947, pp. 116-124.

H. STUART HUGHES, *Oswald Spengler: a Critical Estimate* (New York, 1952).

J. HUIZINGA, *In de Schaduwen van Morgen* (Haarlem, 1935).

J. HUIZINGA, "Twee Worstelaars met den Engel," in *De Gids*, June-July, 1921, p. 454-487, p. 80-109.

ALFRED L. KROEBER, *Configurations of Culture Growth* (U. of Cal., 1944).

TANGYE LEAN: "A Study of History" in *Horizon, a Review of Literature and Art,* January, 1947, pp. 24-55.

PAUL LIGETI, *Der Weg aus dem Chaos* (Munich, 1931).

TH. J. G. LOCHER, "Toynbee's Antwood" in *De Gids,* May, 1948, pp. 98-128.

HENDRIK DE MAN, *Vermassung und Kulturverfall* (Bern, 1951).

MUSEUM OF MODERN ART, New York, *Built in USA since 1932* (New York, 1945).

F. S. C. NORTHROP, *The Meeting of East and West* (New York, 1946).

SIR FLANDERS PETRIE, *The Revolutions of Civilization* (London-New York, 1912).

SIR FLANDERS PETRIE, "History in Art," in *Antiquity,* September, 1931.

K. R. POPPER, *The Open Society and Its Enemies,* II, pp. 237-245.

JAN ROMEIN, *Toynbee's Studie der Geschiedenis* (Bussum, 1948).

JAN ROMEIN, "De Crisis van onze Beschaving in Historisch Perspectief," in *De Nieuwe Stem* I, i, 1946.

WALTER SCHUBART, *Russia and Western Man* (New York, 1950).

D. C. SOMERVELL, *Abridgment of Volumes I-VI of A Study of History by Arnold J. Toynbee* (New York, London, 1947).

PITIRIM SOROKIN, *Social Philosophies of an Age of Crisis* (Boston, 1950).

OSWALD SPENGLER, *Der Untergang des Abendlandes: Umrisse einer Morphologie der Weltgeschichte* (Munchen, 1918-1922). English translation: *The Decline of the West* (New York, 1926-1928).

ED. SPRANGER, *Die Kulturzyklentheorie und das Problem des Kulturverfalls, Sitzungsberichte der Preuss. Akademie der Wissenschaft,* 1926, *Phil. Hist. Klasse,* p. XXXV-LIV.

ARNOLD J. TOYNBEE, *A Study of History,* Vol. I-III (London, 1933); Vol. IV-VI (London, 1939).

ARNOLD J. TOYNBEE, *Civilization on Trial* (New York, 1948).

RALPH E. TURNER, *The Great Cultural Traditions* (New York, 1941).

H. G. WELLS, *The Outline of History* (London, 1920).

Set in Linotype Times Roman
Format by Marguerite Swanton
Manufactured by The Haddon Craftsmen, Inc.
Published by HARPER & BROTHERS, *New York*

Date Due